Aurea Vidyā Collection*

——————— 11 ———————

*For a complete list of Titles, see page 133.

On the Order of Nature

Published by Aurea Vidyā, the Publishing House of Parmenides
Traditional Philosophy Foundation
39 West 88th Street, New York, N.Y. 10024
www.vidya-ashramvidyaorder.org

This book was originally published in Italian as
Parmenide, *Sull'Ordinamento della Natura*, Περί φύσεως, Per
un'ascesi filosofica, a cura di Raphael, by Edizioni Āśram
Vidyā, Roma, Italy 2007

©Āśram Vidyā 2007
English Translation ©Āśram Vidyā 2009
Set in font ©Vidyā 11/13 points by Aurea Vidyā

Printed and bound by Lightning Source Inc. at locations in the
U.S.A. and in the U.K., as shown on the last page.

ISBN   978-1-931406-10-9
Library of Congress Control Number: 2008944221

On the cover: Parmenides
                Cappella Palatina, Parco Archeologico, Velia
                (Elea of ancient Greece), Salerno, Italy.

Parmenides

On the Order of Nature
Περί φύσεως

For a Philosophical Ascesis

Edited by

Raphael
(Āśram Vidyā Order)

AUREA VIDYĀ

TABLE OF CONTENTS

Introduction   9

The Way that leads to Being   17
Being   21
Introduction to the Proem   31

ON THE ORDER OF NATURE   41
Fragment 1, Proem   43
Fragments 2 – 7   49
Preamble to Fragment 8   57
Fragment 8   63
Introduction to the world of appearances   71
Fragments 8 (contd.) – 19   87

Notes to the Fragments   99

Bibliographic Reference   117
Glossary   119
Raphael: Unity of Tradition   127

INTRODUCTION

The date of Parmenides birth is uncertain but, according to the indications of Apollodoros, it can be placed between the sixth and the fifth centuries B.C. Parmenides was born in Magna Graecia, in Elea (today's Velia) located on the coast of Campania south of Paestum, into a family of noble lineage and quite well off. It is known that he governed and gave very good laws to his city (in those days, as it happened, cities were governed by Philosophers), and every year the Eleans pledged their loyalty to those laws. The Pythagorean Ameinias introduced Parmenides to the peace of contemplation, and because of this relationship, Parmenides himself is considered a Pythagorean.

The Eleatic constitutes a "beacon" whose light illumined Plato and even Aristotle, and consequently all the philosophers that followed.

Parmenides laid down several fundamental philosophical principles:

1. The Being as foundation of all the existent

2. The principle of identity, Being is identical to itself (Fr. 4; Fr. 8, 12, 25)

3. The principle of non-contradiction (Fr. 8, 15), which subsequently Aristotle also developed at both the logical and the epistemological level.

4. The principle of a-temporality or eternal present (Fr. 8, 3 and following), while the time aspect (becoming) he puts into δόξα.

5. He has given an initiatory philosophical vision of an experimental order, therefore the Poem cannot leave this vision aside.

This implies that the human entity is put in the conditions to *assimilate* to Being, having the ontological dignity of it.

Parmenides' vision was taken up by Plato and others down to Plotinus and beyond, while staying within the Classical Greek tradition.

With Parmenides began what is called, in more specific terms, true *Philosophy*.

Thus it is not a vision of religious order, the way this term is commonly meant. Religion is, in fact, in the domain of duality, of a passive subject in front of something which is outside of itself, with a marked difference between Creator and creature.

The initiatory way, or way of knowledge, is an active way in which it is recognized that the nature of Being is within us as well, as νοῦσ, essence. In terms of *Vedānta* it corresponds to *paravidyā* (supreme knowledge). Parmenides received the initiation directly from the Goddess Δίκη. The other Goddesses mentioned in the Poem are characterizations, aspects or principles, which are refracted by the one Goddess who, in this case, represents the incarnation of the supreme Truth and the principial cause of manifestation.

The first part of the Poem, which is the most important part, appears to be complete, while that regarding the world of "appearances" is made up of only disconnected fragments, and at times there are just a few words, and therefore difficult to decipher and interpret.

The entire Poem consists of 154 verses. The title "About Nature" (περί φύσεως) is a later addition. It appears for the first time in Simplicius' *De coelo*[1]. Φύσεως (of the text) also means "Natural Order" which corresponds to the Vedāntic *Ṛta*.

It is thought that the theogony of Parmenides was inspired by that of Hesiod, but one cannot give credit to this hypothesis because there are fundamental differences between them[2].

Hesiod, as also Pherecydes of Syrus, proposes that the world was born from the Gods, each with their function; this proposition is a mythical cosmogony, it is an exposition of facts. Parmenides instead expounds a theogony which does not talk about facts. Some points may be considered scientific, while other points deal with astrological aspects. Furthermore, Parmenides places what is born in

[1]   Simplicius, *In De coelo Aristotelis,* 556, 25, D. 28 A 14.

[2]   For a further insight into Hesiod and other relevant aspects, see, Raphael, *Orphism and the Initiatory Tradition*, Aurea Vidyā, New York.

the sphere of "appearances", of phenomena, in δόξα rather than in the sphere of Truth, nevertheless comparing it with the reality of Being.

For the Eleatic the primary aim is the search for the ultimate Truth, beyond cosmogonic factors. Starting from this level of consciousness, Parmenides cannot avoid considering as "appearance" cosmogony itself which operates in time and in history.

From this standpoint, one could say that Parmenides was the first metaphysician in the history of Western philosophy. Metaphysician because he positioned himself beyond time, space and cause. The mortal compared with the immortal may consider himself a συμβεβηκός (accident), something which may or may not be. The non-born (ἀ-γένητος), the ungenerated always stays in its a-temporal aspect.

For the Eleatic the "eternal" has a connotation not of duration, even if indefinite, but of negation of time itself. If Being is ἀ-γένητος it cannot have a temporal succession, since the temporal condition belongs to δόξα.

Moreover, the Eleatic expresses in "dry" terms the reality of Being, the relativity of the phenomena and the fallacy of the opinion of the mortals. Plato calls him "venerable and also fearsome" (*Theaetetus*, 183e). But at the same time this Being unveils itself in the very a-temporal and immortal (νοῦς) dimension of the human entity as the foundation of his existing and being. The being is his aim for liberating himself from the error in which he dwells.

Parmenides in the vision of Being has not connected other dialectical relationships and he has not attributed other meanings except that "Being is and cannot not be". It will be Aristotle's task to give multiple meanings to Being, unmoved mover (τό κινοῦν ἀκίνητον), but Aristotle's philosophy can be considered an Ontology and not pure Metaphysics.

The idea of Being has been the paradigm of the entire Western Philosophy. Both Plato and Aristotle, as it was said, are indebted to the Eleatic, and not only for the idea of Being.

Parmenides does not place the world of becoming in "nothingness" because he himself states that you can neither think nor speak of nothingness.

«Also this you have to learn: how those things which appear must be evaluated in a correct manner»

(Fr. 1, 31-32)

Thus, the error of the mortals consists only in considering the "appearances", or the phenomena, as reality and absolute truths. On the contrary what is needed is to know how to evaluate appearances in the correct manner and see them for what they are in their own nature.

In the field of Western Philosophy Parmenides' influence can be noted by the following:

– A logical dialectical rigor in the exposition

– An existential vision addressed to the human entity

    – A truth coming from on high and not empirically
      theorized or conceptualized by the dianoetic mind

    Such a sacred vision can be revolutionary in a culture that, given the signs of the times, is characterized by a gloomy spiritual, ethical, cultural and political impoverishment[1].

---

[1] Repetitions are there along these various notes. Since this writing is not intended to be an essentially litterary essay, repetitions could be useful to enhance the fixing of the key principles exposed in the Poem.

«... Philosophers are they who draw from that which is always identical to itself, while those who are not fit, but continuously go wandering in mutable things, are not Philosophers...
By nature Philosophers are lovers of the science unveiling the beingness which eternally is, and do not go wandering in cycles of generation and death»

Plato, *Republic*, VI, 484b-485b

The Way that leads to Being

The ὁδός is the "way" traveled by Parmenides, but it is Δίκη who awakens the consciousness of the would-be initiate to the supreme Truth. And it is in the descent that Parmenides, once realized, offers Truth to the world of humans and above all to those who begin to feel, not just theoretically but operatively, to be "children of Being" more than children of appearances. Δίκη was able to awaken in Parmenides the consciousness of Being because a mortal has in himself also the "thread" linking him to Being, and therefore, as mentioned earlier, the mortal's *Essence* is of the nature of Being. Δίκη would not, otherwise, be able to awaken what is not in our nature or what is not in a state of potential.

Plato then will talk of ἀνάμνησις, a reminiscence of metaphysical order and not just a simple historical memory of the empirical. And so, in the "Myth of the Cave", he indicates a *way* to be journeyed in order to leave the world of shadows, of simulacra, and contemplate in a direct way the solar Light of true knowledge. Then who has "contemplated" can return to the world of the non-awakened and stimulate to the consciousness of Being at least those who are ready to listen.

For regaining consciousness of what one is, there
is always a path, a way to be traveled, a "philosophical
ascesis" to be considered. While on the other hand, as
far as what emerges from the few fragments, with regard
to the polarity of Day and Night, the *Daimon* expounds
a vision of what the world of appearances represents, and
also gives an operative process of both the macrocosm
and the microcosm:

> «As appearance, these things are originated and in the
> future will develop to then have an end»
>
> (Fr. 19, 1-2)

Here Parmenides introduces the theme of time: for
this reason it is possible to affirm along with Plato: time
is the shadow, the image of the a-temporal.

Thus, we need to distinguish between the two conditions: one addressed to the subject to be awakened, the
other to the transient object that also needs to be known.

The journey of the ὁδός leads to the unveiling of the
supreme or ultimate Truth which holds numerous other
(πολύφημος) cognitive possibilities within itself. This
way is the one which is certain because it is indicated by
Δίκη who is the incarnation of the Truth, while those in
the world of the mortals, who have not journeyed on the
Way, can offer just opinions (Plato speaks of *filodoxi*, not
of philosophers lovers of σοφία or φρόνησις).

The scholar Jean Zafiropulo, who is well-versed in the things of the Eleatic school, maintains that Parmenides, being a chosen one and having traveled the όδός, talks to chosen ones, and so it is with this perspective that the entire Poem has to be comprehended.[1]

We are in agreement with this thesis. It can be added that Parmenides, as it was touched upon earlier, talks to true philosophers who want to follow the όδός traveled by the Eleatic.

It is possible to believe that Parmenides put his attention above all on the όδός, that the entire Poem is the unfolding of a Way to be traveled, an operative path, coming to an end with the philosophical initiation.

The Proem is of extreme importance because it indicates the όδός traveled by the Eleatic, thanks to which he was then able to offer the fruit of his Awakening. Without the όδός he could not have touched the apex of supreme Truth, in this case assimilated to Δίκη. The unveiling of the entire teaching of Parmenides above all implies and presupposes the όδός. Were the Proem to be excluded, all the discourse that follows could not be interpreted according to the intent of the Eleatic.

From what has come before, one can say that the philosophy of Parmenides is not a dialectic aimed at demonstrating some point of view of his according to statements

---

[1] Unless otherwise footnoted, for all Bibliographic Reference see page 117.

from which to draw rational conclusions, therefore not a conceptual philosophy.

Parmenides indicates one *Way* only to be followed, whose knowledge has to resolve itself in a state of consciousness (Fr. 1, 26-27):

«...not an adverse Moira sent you to travel this way (ὁδός) – which is far from the path traveled by men»

Being

In Parmenides' Being duality is unthinkable, so is multiplicity in whatever form one wants to apply it. Being is not an ontological entity, or a cause of production, but something more.

Being is not Aristotle's "unmoved mover" from which the chain of movements is set in motion, as a first cause determining specific effects[1]. It is not even the θεός of Plato, as the God-person, even if Plato goes beyond ontology.

Parmenides' Being is immutable, whole in its entirety, it remains indivisible in its identity, beyond time, space and cause, because:

> «Nor was it ever, nor will it be, since it is now all together one, continuous. Which birth (γέννα) for it, in fact, will you be looking for?»
>
> (Fr. 8, 5-6)

> «Nor from Being will the vigor of a certitude allow that anything be born which be close to it...»
>
> (Fr. 8, 12-13)

---

[1] Aristotle, *Physics*, VIII, 7; and, *Metaphysics*, XII, 6.

This Being does not admit that there is a second in itself or in front of itself.

From this perspective it can be compared to the One-without-a-second of *Advaita Vedānta*.

The Non-born[1] cannot have a birth because a change of nature is impossible.

> «...from them [world of names and forms][2] he stays away, thinking that through what is created the Uncreated cannot be attained»
>
> (*Muṇḍaka Upaniṣad*, II, 1, 12)

> «On one hand, in fact, there is being, driven here and there, exposed to all sorts of change, and in every place, and which is better called "becoming" rather than "being". On the other, there is Being, eternal, undivided, always same to itself, which has no birth nor does it die, set in no region, place or support of its own, does not emerge from one place to enter another, but stays fast in itself»
>
> (Plotinus, *Enneads*, VI, 5, 2)[3]

Nor can it be stated that *physis* is *within* Being, nor that it *is* Being. *Physis* is of the nature of movement, of action, and therefore of cause and necessity, while Being

---

[1] For the *Ajativāda* see, Gauḍapāda, *Māṇḍūkyakārikā* , The Metaphysical Path of Vedānta. Aurea Vidyā. New York.

[2] Square brackets along the text are ours.

[3] See also, Plato, *Sophist*, 248A; and, *Symposium*, 211A.

is not bound by necessity, is immobile, complete, non-born (see below). If Being is indivisible, how can it allow multiplicity to enter within itself? If Being is unity, a Whole (οὖλον), it cannot include within itself that which is fragmentary. If Being is Truth it cannot have in itself τὰ δοκοῦντα. Nor can Being, as it is eternal, depend from the polarity Day-Night which has an end. It can be stated that Being is, also in absence of Day-Night, since Being is in fact the Non-born.

Nor, again, can there be next to the Non-born another non-born beside it. Nor can something be found in It that is less, such as the becoming of things which, in *comparison* to Being, *is not*.

In Being there cannot be both Day and Night contemporaneously because they invalidate each other. Nor can it be that one part of Being *be* while the other part remains as simple "appearance" or phenomenon, because this would go towards invalidating the unity of Being which is non-born. Nor, therefore, can Being be split temporarily, so that one part would remain immobile and the other mobile and conditioned by the temporal process, because Being is not divisible, it is totally whole, it is ταὐτόν τ' ἐν ταὐτῶι, identical to itself (Fr. 8, 29). It can be said that Being represents the eternal unchangeable *screen* on which the chiaroscuro effects of manifestation intertwine.

Parmenides states that Being must be «...entirely whole, or not exist at all» (Fr. 8, 29). At this point we may ask ourselves the question: Can the Being of Parmenides be considered as transcending Day-Night?

Drawing from what he expounds in his Poem, the Eleatic does not propose a pantheism by identifying Being with the world of appearances. The latter does not possess the properties of the former (as it will be said when illustrating the apparent-manifest). As matters stand, Being transcends Day-Night but, at the same time, does not establish with Day-Night a duality that is irreconcilable, because having a founding function, Being gives Day-Night the possibility to exist and to be what it is.

There is not, therefore, an absolute transcendence, completely detached from the temporal context. However it is also true that the non-born Being does not necessitate Day-Night (which is born) to be what it is, while the latter without the former cannot have a raison d'être. One is eternal, the other has birth and end, appears and disappears, and, therefore, as Plato says, it cannot be put, for dignity and potency, on the same level with Being.

If one starts from these root principles, Fragment 9 of the δόξα also can be explained in the sense that both Light and Night, to which these names have been given, have Being as a metaphysical foundation. However while the ὀδός of Light leads to Being beyond causality, the other path leads to the world of "appearances" and opinion.

> «everything is evenly full of Light and dark Night both even because neither with one nor with the other is the nothingness»
>
> (Fr. 9, 3-4)

Since Light and Darkness represent the intelligible and the sensible plane respectively, both possess a degree of truth. To put Light and Darkness on the same plane is not reasonable. Parmenides himself could have used a single term for Being as well as for δόξα. In Platonic terms they can be named intelligible plane and sensible plane, as said earlier.

In this way the Goddess expounds both the Truth leading to Being and the opinion of the mortals leading to error.

Neither can Light and Darkness be convertible.

The world of name and form may appear as reality to the dianoetic mind, but νόησις is able to *comprehend* its true nature. In the *Vedānta* too it is stated that the world of appearance is not like the "horns of a hare" or the "child of a barren woman", i.e. it is not an absolute negation.

Viewing the problem from this stand point it is not acceptable that the world of *doxa* (which has an end) be also Being (which is eternal) as if this one contained within itself ἀλήθεια and δόξα, the ὄν and the μὴ ὄν like an immense receptacle, or a large pan, in which are stirred both Being and phenomenon-appearance. A reading of a purely metaphysical order can connect the Being of the Eleatic (the non-born, the non-become, etc.) to the One-Good of Plato, the One of Plotinus and the *nirguṇa Brahman* of the *Vedānta*.

In a *sūtra* of the *pali* Canon there is a quotation in which a monk asks the Buddha if something exists or nothing at all exists. The Buddha responds:

«There is that which is not born, not become, not created, and not conditioned. If there were not that, which is not born, not become, not made, not conditioned, there could be no escape from that which is born, become, made, conditioned»[1]

(*Udana*, 73)

«If nothing eternal existed, the becoming could not exist either»

(Aristotle, *Metaphysics* B4, 999 b 5-6)

«Which birth (γέννα) for it, in fact, will you be looking for? How and in what way would it have grown?»

(Fr. 8, 6-7)

«This is the eternal greatness of *Brahman*: it does not increase nor does it diminish»[2]

(*Bṛhadāraṇyaka Upaniṣad*, IV, IV, 23)

«...He will, all of a sudden, perceive a Beauty of its nature stupendous and precisely that, oh Socrates, for which all the earlier pains were endured, that which is first of all eternal, which does not become and does not perish, does not grow and does not diminish»[3]

(Plato, *Symposium*, 210e-211a)

---

[1] *Buddhist Canon*, *Short Discourses*, Volume II, Udana VIII. Edited by Pio Filippani-Ronconi. UTET. Torino 1968. (Italian Edition).

[2] *Bṛhadāraṇyaka Upaniṣad*, Edizioni Āśram Vidyā, Roma. (Italian Edition).

[3] Plato, *Complete Works*, edited by Giovanni Pugliese Caratelli, translation by Emilio Martini, Sansoni Editore. Firenze 1974. (Italian Edition).

Being, since it is non-born, cannot contain in itself spacial or temporal elements, nor can it be reborn as it already exists, nor can it have factors of growth or decrease; these categories belong to what is born.

On the other hand, given that Being is all that is, and nothing is left outside of itself other than itself, it can be said that all that does not fall in the σήματα, in those "indicating signs", is phenomenon (Fr. 8, 8-2).

It has been said earlier that Being does not represent the Principle from which all proceeds. Fragment 8, 12-13 is repeated:

«Nor from Being will the vigor of a certitude allow that anything be born which be close to it...»[1]

The birth of the world occurs through the *Daimon* without involving Being, the Non-born. It is she who is the principial cause, it is she who has an ontological stature.

If one does come out of the temporal succession, the eternal present, or timelessness, cannot be comprehended. However, Being and non-being, the immobile and the mobile cannot be two opposing factors. They are not two absolutes, but the immobile, the immutable is that which is superior to the mobile-becoming.

As it was said earlier, the human entity having within itself the 'spark' of Being, which is its essence, is brought back to Being, in the way a sun ray unites with the sun.

---

[1] For the cause of manifestation see the Chapter, "Introduction to the world of becoming".

And hence the ὁδός that leads to Being. The ἐὸν of the
Eleatic represents, therefore, the metaphysical foundation
of the all existing. It is that because of which Day and
Night, with all that these terms imply, can emerge into
existence. However the ἐὸν is beyond Day and Night, these
can be considered οὐσία, according to Plato's meaning,
they are the polar cause that determines effects.

«...It is *Brahman*, and due to It all is manifested, but
It is not manifested by anything...»

«Realize that *Brahman* whose splendor illumines the
sun and the other stars, but is not illumined by their
light, [that *Brahman*] only thanks to which all this
[universe] is manifested»[1]

(*Ātmabodha*, 61)

Parmenides invites us to observe the becoming-sen-
sible with the "eye" of Being, and not with the formal
physical eye which identifies with the object.

«...the blind sighted eye, the ringing ear...»

(Fr. 7, 4)

Given its limit, the sensory eye is forced to see, think
and conceptualize the becoming of things as a real event.
Hence the path of error by which Being is mistaken for
the appearance. And all this is consolidated by «...habit,
born of many experiences» (Fr. 7, 3).

---

[1] Śaṅkara, *Ātmabodha*. Aurea Vidyā. New York.

The subject of the Eleatic is distinct (not opposed), is autonomous (as it is non-born) from the visible object (which is born). If the human subject were to rise to the Vision of Parmenides, not granting absoluteness to the idol of the exclusively dianoetic and opinionated thinking, and were to go back within himself in order to awaken νόησις and unveil ἀλήθεια, then Parmenides could constitute his salvation at various levels of manifestation.

If man were to recognize that he is something more than a simple sensible form, and that he belongs to a lineage greatly superior to that which he thinks he is descending from, rather than putting his attention on the external object, he could put his attention on the subject, which is himself, and is the true Δαίμων of his own destiny.

«The wise philosopher... should not dissipate his mind into many words, futile resonance of voice»[1]

(*Bṛhadāraṇyaka Upaniṣad*, IV, IV, 21)

«Τοῦτο τοίνυν τὸ τὴν ἀλήθειαν παρέχον τοῖς γιγνωσ-κομένοις καὶ τῷ γιγνώσκοντι τὴν δύναμιν ἀποδιδὸν τὴν τοῦ ἀγαθοῦ ἰδέαν φάθι εἶναι· αἰτίαν δ' ἐπιστήμης οὖσαν καὶ ἀληθείας, ὡς γιγνωσκομένην μὲν διανοοῦ, οὕτω δὲ καλῶν ἀμφοτέρων ὄντων, γνώσεώς τε καὶ ἀληθείας, ἄλλο καὶ κάλλιον ἔτι τούτων ἡγούμενος αὐτὸ ὀρθῶς ἡγήσῃ· ἐπιστήμην δὲ καὶ ἀλήθειαν, ὥσπερ ἐκεῖ φῶς τε καὶ ὄψιν ἡλιοειδῆ μὲν νομίζειν ὀρθόν, ἥλιον δ' ἡγεῖσθαι οὐκ ὀρθῶς ἔχει, οὕτω καὶ ἐνταῦθα ἀγαθοειδῆ μὲν νομίζειν ταῦτ' ἀμφότερα ὀρθόν, ἀγαθὸν

---

[1] *Bṛhadāraṇyaka Upaniṣad*. Op. cit.

δὲ ἡγεῖσθαι ὁπότερον αὐτῶν οὐκ ὀρθόν, ἀλλ' ἔτι
μειζόνως τιμητέον τὴν τοῦ ἀγαθοῦ ἕξιν».

«This, therefore, which provides the known things with
Truth, and the knower with the faculty of knowing
them, you have to say is the Idea of Good. And since
it is cause of knowledge and truth, consider it know-
able. And since they are both beautiful, knowledge
and truth, if you will maintain that to be different from
these and even more beautiful, you will be in the right.
And while science and truth, like light and sight are
right to be considered similar to the Sun, but not to
be considered Sun, likewise it is right to hold those
both similar to the Good, but to maintain that both,
one and the other, are the Good is not right because
the condition of the Good must be considered even
greater»[1]

(*Politeia*, VI, 508e - 509a)

Being for Parmenides is not knowledge but the foundation on which both opinion and noetic knowledge (γνῶσις)
are able to be and to express themselves. The two aspects
are qualities, but Being, as is proposed, is beyond quality
and quantity.

[1]   Plato, *All the Writings*, edited by Giovanni Reale. Bompiani.
Milano. (Italian Edition).

Introduction to the Proem

The Proem represents a precise initiation into Supreme Knowledge. "Supreme" in that it refers to the ultimate Reality from which all existing entities, of whatever nature and degree, depend and beyond which there can be no other reality. A knowledge (*paravidyā*, as it is called in the *Vedānta*) which disperses the error in which the mortals fall. Having already traveled the way of opinative knowledge (*aparavidyā* of the *Vedānta*) and having recognized that there is no "true certainty" by this way, because it is contradictory, Parmenides is led by the unveiling maidens, daughters of the Sun and the Light, into the presence of the Goddess Δίκη. The "door" (of initiation) having been knocked, it opens to introduce the would-be initiate into the "Hall of Wisdom" and to receive the philosophical initiation.

A door which can be opened only by those who are worthy of opening it, hence the perplexity of the Goddess who wants to first ascertain the qualification of the would-be initiate.

In the Orphic Tradition the would-be initiate is bared by the guardians who protect the two ways.

«To the right of the houses of Hades you will find a
   wellspring,
Next to which a white cypress stands tall...
Do not even approach this wellspring
Further you will find the cold waters that flow from
   the lake of Mnemosyne
In front of this spring are Guardians who will ask you
   what are you searching for»[1]

The door is a symbol of a philosophical-initiatory
iter. The would-be initiate always finds a door on which
he must knock and is accompanied by he, or those, who
have instructed him on both the Doctrine and the formal
and ethical behavior.

Given his philosophical approach, Parmenides is
connected to the Pythagorean Tradition and thus to the
Orphic Tradition and to the Eleusinian Sacred Mysteries,
to which Plato himself is connected. These Mysteries
are the expression of the Apollonian vision (Apollo from
ά-πόλλων = not many, non-dual).

«But we are troubled and insecure about the words
that we have to adopt for the Ineffable and we invent
words with the desire to call him, in a way possible
to us, to ourselves... Therefore also the Pythagoreans,

---

[1] *Gold-leaf tablet,* from a tomb in Pharsalus (Museum of Volos),
Thessaly, Greece. Laid in a bronze vase dateable to the second half of the
IV Century b.c. For the Orphic Tradition see: Raphael, *Orphism and the
Initiatory Tradition.* Aurea Vidyā. New York.

among themselves, symbolically define it as Apollo to negate (ἀποφάσει) multiplicity (τῶν πολλῶν)»

(Plotinus, *Enneads*, V, 5, VI)

It is maintained that Parmenides was disciple of the Pythagorean Ameinias, hence his connection with Pythagoras and therefore with Orphism.

Parmenides himself is considered a Pythagorean. Diogenes Laertius[1], with reference to Sotion, states that Parmenides had ties with the Pythagorean Ameinias, son of Diochaitas, who was poor, but endowed of great virtue. Parmenides followed him also because he believed that despite his great knowledge, he was humble. On Ameinias's death, Parmenides erected a votive sacellum, which indicates the special relationship they enjoyed. Always according to Diogenes, it was Ameinias more than Xenophanes of Colophon, who introduced him to the tranquillity of philosophical life.

The door, by opening, brings Parmenides onto the "Main Way", where the Δαίμον-Truth, introducing the would-be initiate and leading him by the hand, bestows upon him affable words: «Oh young companion, led by mares and immortal charioteers». This shows that the latter belong to the intelligible plane (Way of Light) and thus are worthy of leading towards the door a would-be initiate to the supreme Truth.

---

[1] Diogenes Laertius, *Lives of the Philosophers*, IX, 21.

«...for no adverse Moira sent you to travel this path
(ὁδός) – which is far from the way traveled by men»

(Fr. 1, 26-27)

By going through the door he passes from the world
of Night to the world of Light, of illumination (ἀλήθεια),
that is from the sensible world to the intelligible world (see
Fr. 1, 8-10). The Goddess is Δίκη, the personification, in
this case, of the ultimate Truth. It should be noticed that
the Goddess expresses the intelligible truth as opposed
to the Goddesses-Muses of which both Homer and even
Hesiod talked about, which are Muses belonging to a
lesser plane.

Moreover, Parmenides not only has "heard", not only
has realized what he heard («In fact, the same is to think
[know] and be [that of which one has thought]» (Fr. 3, 1),
but coming back to the world of men who "err", he has
also brought a message of salvation, as some scholars of
the Eleatic have maintained.

In the philosophical asceticism, unlike simple, dis-
cursive and rational philosophy, what has been "heard",
and known, is lived, and thus knowledge becomes emi-
nently cathartic. There is then a shift from a dianoetic
conceptualization to a knowledge that "does not think",
but unveils by itself without a hurdle, a silent knowledge
that originates from other dimensions of the entity itself.

If philosophy does not touch the *consciousness* of the
human entity to awaken him to the world of Principles, it

stays as mental exercise, as an end in itself although, at this level, it may have a preliminary value.

The Eleatic is among those "thinkers" who *do not think* the truth. He does not expound a thinking or a philosophizing of his own but, as mentioned already, he "heard" it (like the Vedic *Ṛṣi*) and presented it to the world of men. It is thus a truth coming from on High to help the beings who «go wandering, two-headed men... who know nothing» (Fr. 6, 4-5) and therefore uncertainty that guides them.

This is a message, directed to those who want to "knock" on that door. By following Parmenides' teaching, they can open it as he did.

According to the scholar Zafiropulo:

«...Le prologue... simbolise sans aucun doute possible l'initiation qui était de règle dans la secte pythagoricienne... Ainsi se trouve fixé l'esprit dans le quelle tout le poème doit être entendu»

«The prologue symbolizes, without any possible doubt, the initiation that was practised as a rule in the Pythagorean circle... This way the spirit in which the entire Poem has to be comprehended is set»

If the Proem is removed, Parmenides' message is incomplete and the entire work cannot be comprehended.

Divine law (Θέμις), Divine Justice, as universal Order (Δίκη), and Moira (Μοῖρα) as Destiny, or the Law which must be applied, are personifications of Principles, and in this specific case, can be expressions of the very Goddess Δίκη, as she personifies the supreme reality-Truth and causal principle of Day-Night.

«...And the appearances of the mortals in which there is no true certainty» (Fr. 1, 30) not possessing a stable truth, because they do not rest on the *continuum* nor on cognitive firmness, are contradictory.

«Nevertheless also this you have to learn: how the things that appear must in the correct way be evaluated» (Fr. 1, 31-32) i.e. what sort of validity the appearances and the opinions of the mortals must have. Throughout the Poem this thought is taken up again.

Faced with erroneous evaluations, in which the opinion of the mortals may fall, Parmenides' indications are incontrovertible and allow no way out through any dialectical dianoetic escape. Tò ὄv is and cannot not be; the μὴ ὄv, opposed to τò ὄv, is not and will never be; therefore one can neither think nor speak of nihilistic nothingness.

Day and Night are just a phenomenon-appearance of the temporal becoming, perceivable as object. From this perspective it can be asserted that by making the world of becoming absolute one does not attain the reality of Being. As much as one wants to transform or rectify the "second" (and how many times this is done), it will continue to be the prisoner of the contradictory and conflictual time[1].

---

[1] See, "Introduction to the world of appearances-*doxa*", on page 71 of this text.

What matters – and this is believed to be Parmenides' revelation – is not to go along the way of δόξα on which there is no "true certainty", but to fix oneself, beyond any diaonetic vision, in the state of Being, in that in which one is.

Parmenides is τὸν φρονεῖν βροτοὺσ οδώσαντα: he who has introduced the mortals to the straight path of wisdom.

μόνος δ' ἔτι μῦθος ὁδοῖο
λείπεται ὡς ἔστιν· ταύτηι δ' ἐπὶ σήματ' ἔασι
πολλὰ μάλ', ὡς ἀγένητον ἐὸν καὶ ἀνώλεθρόν ἐστιν,
ἔστι γὰρ οὐλομελές τε καὶ ἀτρεμὲς ἠδ' ἀτέλεστον·

«Only one discourse is left about the Way that it is.
On this way there are revealing signs in great numbers:
that Being is non-born (ἀγένητον),
incorruptible (ἀνώλεθρόν), in fact it is entirely whole,
immobile and without end (ἀτέλεστον)»

ΠΑΡΜΕΝΙΔΟΥ

ΠΕΡΙ ΦΥΣΕΩΣ

PARMENIDES

ON THE ORDER OF NATURE

ἵπποι ταί με φέρουσιν, ὅσον τ’ ἐπὶ θυμὸς ἱκάνοι,
πέμπον, ἐπεί μ’ ἐς ὁδὸν βῆσαν πολύφημον ἄγουσαι
δαίμονες, ἣ κατὰ πάντ’ ἄστη φέρει εἰδότα φῶτα·
τῆι φερόμην· τῆι γάρ με πολύφραστοι φέρον ἵπποι
ἅρμα τιταίνουσαι, κοῦραι δ’ ὁδὸν ἡγεμόνευον.   5
ἄξων δ’ ἐν χνοίηισιν ἵει σύριγγος ἀυτήν
αἰθόμενος (δοιοῖς γὰρ ἐπείγετο δινωτοῖσιν
κύκλοις ἀμφοτέρωθεν), ὅτε σπερχοίατο πέμπειν
Ἡλιάδες κοῦραι, προλιποῦσαι δώματα Νυκτός,

---

[1] For the Greek text we follow the reading of Hermann Diels and Walther Kranz, *Die Fragmmente der Vorsokratiker.* Refer to page 117.

Fragment 1

PROEM

The mares that take me according to my will
they carry me after they had guided me on the Way
that unveils many a knowledge,
[Way] that belongs to divinity and leads the man
who knows through all cities [or everywhere].
There I was taken, in fact, there they led me wise
mares
5   pulling my chariot while maidens were showing
the way (ὁδός).
The axle red hot in the hubs was shrieking and hissing,
for it was driven on either side
by two whirling wheels
as the maidens daughters of the Sun hastened having left
the house of Night,

εἰς φάος, ὠσάμεναι κράτων ἄπο χερσὶ καλύπτρας.   10
  ἔνθα πύλαι Νυκτός τε καὶ Ἤματός εἰσι κελεύθων,
καί σφας ὑπέρθυρον ἀμφὶς ἔχει καὶ λάινος οὐδός·
αὐταὶ δ᾽ αἰθέριαι πλῆνται μεγάλοισι θυρέτροις·
τῶν δὲ Δίκη πολύποινος ἔχει κληῖδας ἀμοιβούς.
τὴν δὴ παρφάμεναι κοῦραι μαλακοῖσι λόγοισιν.   15
πεῖσαν ἐπιφραδέως, ὥς σφιν βαλανωτὸν ὀχῆα
ἀπτερέως ὤσειε πυλέων ἄπο· ταὶ δὲ θυρέτρων
χάσμ᾽ ἀχανὲς ποίησαν ἀναπτάμεναι πολυχάλκους
ἄξονας ἐν σύριγξιν ἀμοιβαδὸν εἰλίξασαι
γόμφοις καὶ περόνῃσιν ἀρηρότε· τῇ ῥα δι᾽ αὐτέων   20
ἰθὺς ἔχον κοῦραι κατ᾽ ἀμαξιτὸν ἅρμα καὶ ἵππους.
  καί με θεὰ πρόφρων ὑπεδέξατο, χεῖρα δὲ χειρί
δεξιτερὴν ἕλεν, ὧδε δ᾽ ἔπος φάτο καί με προσηύδα·
ὦ κοῦρ᾽ ἀθανάτοισι συνάορος ἡνιόχοισιν,

10   for the house of Light, pushing back with their hands the
veils from their heads.
      There is the gate of the Ways of Day and Night,
bounded by a threshold and a stone lintel,
high in the ether space and supported by two great
doors.
Of these Δίκη, Goddess of the nemesis, guards the keys
which open and close in turn.
15   The maidens, with gentle words,
persuading the Goddess to open, without hesitation, the
gates removing the bar
and the gates at once opening
left a wide gap between the leaves, swinging
the bronze hinges on their axes
20   secured with studs and pins.   And here immediately
through the door
the maidens steered the chariot and the mares
straight on the road.
      The Goddess kindly welcomed me and took
my right hand in hers,
and addressing me she uttered so:
«Oh young companion, led by the mares and the immortal
charioteers,

ἵπποις ταί σε φέρουσιν ἱκάνων ἡμέτερον δῶ,   25
χαῖρ', ἐπεὶ οὔτι σε μοῖρα κακὴ προὔπεμπε νέεσθαι
τήνδ' ὁδόν (ἦ γὰρ ἀπ' ἀνθρώπων ἐκτὸς πάτου ἐστίν),
ἀλλὰ θέμις τε δίκη τε. χρεὼ δέ σε πάντα πυθέσθαι
ἠμὲν Ἀληθείης εὐκυκλέος ἀτρεμὲς ἦτορ
ἠδὲ βροτῶν δόξας, ταῖς οὐκ ἔνι πίστις ἀληθής.   30
ἀλλ' ἔμπης καὶ ταῦτα μαθήσεαι, ὡς τὰ δοκοῦντα
χρῆν δοκίμως εἶναι διὰ παντὸς πάντα περ ὄντα.

25   you come to our home:
        rejoice, for no adverse Moira
        sent you to travel this path – which is far from the way
        traveled by men –
        but Θέμις and Δίκη. You must comprehend all:
        the firm heart of the well-rounded Truth[1]
30   and the appearances of mortals in which there is no true
        certainty.
        Nevertheless this also you have to learn: how things
        that appear (δοκοῦντα)
        must in a correct way be evaluated.

---

[1] For the Notes to the Fragments, see page 101 and following.

2

εἰ δ' ἄγ' ἐγὼν ἐρέω, κόμισαι δὲ σὺ μῦθον ἀκούσας,
αἵπερ ὁδοὶ μοῦναι διζήσιός εἰσι νοῆσαι·
ἡ μὲν ὅπως ἔστιν τε καὶ ὡς οὐκ ἔστι μὴ εἶναι,
Πειθοῦς ἐστι κέλευθος (Ἀληθείηι γὰρ ὀπηδεῖ),
ἡ δ' ὡς οὐκ ἔστιν τε καὶ ὡς χρεών ἐστι μὴ εἶναι,   5
τὴν δή τοι φράζω παναπευθέα ἔμμεν ἀταρπόν·
οὔτε γὰρ ἂν γνοίης τό γε μὴ ἐὸν (οὐ γὰρ ἀνυστόν)
οὔτε φράσαις.

Fragment 2

But come, I will tell you; hear and welcome my
revelation (μῦθον)
which are the ways of search, the only fit ones to be
traveled:
one, that it *is* and that (ὡς) it cannot not be
[this] is the way of Persuasion, in fact Ἀληθείηι γὰρ
ὀπηδεῖ: it follows truth
the other that (ὡς) it *is not* and that (ὡς) it must not be,
and this I say to you is a way that cannot be known;
in fact you could not know what *is not* because
it is not possible
nor can you express it (οὔτε φράσαις)².

5

3

... τὸ γὰρ αὐτὸ νοεῖν ἐστίν τε καὶ εἶναι

4

    λεῦσσε δ᾽ ὅμως ἀπεόντα νόωι παρεόντα βεβαίως·
οὐ γὰρ ἀποτμήξει τὸ ἐὸν τοῦ ἐόντος ἔχεσθαι
οὔτε σκιδνάμενον πάντηι πάντως κατὰ κόσμον
οὔτε συνιστάμενον.

Fragment 3

In fact, the same is to think [know] and to be [that of which one has thought][3].

Fragment 4

Observe with noetic intuition, as absent things (ἀπεόντα) are, according to truth, present as well;[4]
in fact you will not be able to cut off Being (τὸ ἐὸν) from
the connection with Being [itself] (ἐόντος)
not in a complete [cosmic] dissolution
nor when it condenses.

5

ξυνὸν δέ μοί ἐστιν,
ὁππόθεν ἄρξωμαι· τόθι γὰρ πάλιν ἵξομαι αὖθις.

6

χρὴ τὸ λέγειν τε νοεῖν τ᾽ ἐὸν ἔμμεναι· ἔστι γὰρ εἶναι,
μηδὲν δ᾽ οὐκ ἔστιν· τά σ᾽ ἐγὼ φράζεσθαι ἄνωγα.
πρώτης γάρ σ᾽ ἀφ᾽ ὁδοῦ ταύτης διζήσιος < εἴργω >,
αὐτὰρ ἔπειτ᾽ ἀπὸ τῆς, ἣν δὴ βροτοὶ εἰδότες οὐδὲν
πλάττονται, δίκρανοι· ἀμηχανίη γὰρ ἐν αὐτῶν   5

Fragment 5

To me irrelevant is
the starting point, there again in fact shall I return[5].

Fragment 6

There must be saying and intuiting that Being be: in
fact Being is,
nothingness is not [nor can it be thought nor intuited] and
these I invite you to ponder.
Therefore, from this way of search I keep you far, but
then also from the way along which the mortals who
know nothing
5   go wandering, two-headed [δίκρανοι, in the text]; in fact
indecisiveness

στήθεσιν ἰθύνει πλακτὸν νόον· οἱ δὲ φοροῦνται
κωφοὶ ὁμῶς τυφλοί τε, τεθηπότες, ἄκριτα φῦλα,
οἷς τὸ πέλειν τε καὶ οὐκ εἶναι ταὐτὸν νενόμισται
κοὐ ταὐτόν, πάντων δὲ παλίντροπός ἐστι κέλευθος.

7

οὐ γὰρ μήποτε τοῦτο δαμῆι εἶναι μὴ ἐόντα·
ἀλλὰ σὺ τῆσδ᾽ ἀφ᾽ ὁδοῦ διζήσιος εἶργε νόημα
μηδέ σ᾽ ἔθος πολύπειρον ὁδὸν κατὰ τήνδε βιάσθω,
νωμᾶν ἄσκοπον ὄμμα καὶ ἠχήεσσαν ἀκουήν
καὶ γλῶσσαν, κρῖναι δὲ λόγωι πολύδηριν ἔλεγχον   5
ἐξ ἐμέθεν ῥηθέντα.

in their hearts leads their senseless mind. They are guided,
both deaf and blind, beings devoid of intellect
for who (τε καὶ οὐκ εἶναι) Being and non-being are
deemed the same (ταὐτόν)
and not the same, and for them of all things there is a
way turning in the opposite direction[6].

Fragment 7

Why ever be enforced the existence of things that are not.
From this way of search keep your mind away,
and not let habit, born of many an experience, drag you
along this way
turning the blind sighted eye, the ringing ear[7]
and word [itself]; judge instead by reason the refutation[8]
5   which to you in many a talk, I expounded»[9].

Preamble to Fragment 8

We have seen earlier (Fr. 6) that there are three ways: one of the non-being in absolute terms; this way (and this is obvious) cannot be traveled owing to its insubstantial nature of non-reality.

The other way is that of opinion and of appearance, things do appear but they are not the foundation that underlies appearance.

Concerning this, there is an example which is highly significant. It is expounded by Gauḍapāda and Śaṅkara, the two philosophers and mystics, codifiers of *Advaita Vedānta*. At dusk a wayfarer along a country road sees a snake. He is afraid to go past it, stops and turns back. But there is no snake, just a twisted rope somebody left behind (see also Plato's "Myth of the Cave"). The *sensory tools* were mistaken, the rope is reality-Truth on which the wayfarer has superimposed a deceptive *opinion*.

It can be said that he has mistaken the rope for a snake or, in our case, reality for temporal phenomenon which gets superimposed onto Being-Reality. This is the "eye" Parmenides talks about, unable to see, and the ear unable to hear. Hence a philosophy and a truth which are reductive, postulating a world just of contingent phenomena and devoid of universal truth.

And when the erroneous and false truth, fruit of «...habit, born of many experiences» crystallizes, it is not easy to modify it or to remove it.

«...For it will be names all of those things the mortals decided convinced that they were true [i.e. absolute]»

(Fr. 8, 38-39)

The names are for communication sake, for verbal relation. What can be true for a determined set of co-ordinates might not be so in other systems of co-ordinates. You cannot "fix" what appears and disappears, give it substance, or a being, for by the time you named it, it has slipped through your hands already.

Hence the drama of the entity who deems valid what he "sees and hears", fruit of simple thoughtless habit.

«Like children's playthings are the beliefs of men»

(Heraclitus, Fragment 63)

This Fragment by Heraclitus is very important and truthful. Children in fact express themselves, obviously, through the sensory apparatus (the five senses) because their *logos* is still at the potential state, and what they see and touch is therefore true, and real. But there is a culture of phenomenalism, no longer product of children, that philosophically remains as a child. The serious error, though, does not lie in deriving knowledge from the sensory experience Parmenides is talking about, but rather in stopping at this false and opinative conviction. Thus crystallizing and casting in stone unsubstantial opinions and the "temporal world of appearing", a world that rolls by, sweeping away all of the mortals' convictions to reach its end (Fr. 19 of the *doxa*). Hence Heraclitus states:

«In the same river we enter and enter not, we are and are not»

(Heraclitus, Fragment 16)

When one sees a tree and you describe what appears to the senses, a concept of that tree has been formulated, but if one thinks to have "comprehended" the tree for what it really is you are very far from the truth.

In other words, we have given an opinion, but the *essence* (τὸ τί ἐστι) of the tree has not been grasped. Often we are content with an opinion without going any deeper into the problem and, further, if we are completely identified with our opinion we end up excluding any other possibility that might be put forward.

Hence the drama of the man that recognizes what he "sees and hears" as fruit of the habit of which Parmenides is talking about.

However Parmenides also teaches:

«...how things that appear must in a correct way be evaluated»

(Fr. 1, 31-32)

And he makes us comprehend that not having a foundation in itself, opinion refers to something else that lies behind it.

Thus, if the first way is not and cannot ever be and the second way does not respond to the ultimate truth that finds in itself its own raison d'être, then it follows that:

«...Only one discourse is left about the Way (ὁδός) [that] it is. On this way there are revealing signs in great numbers...»

(Fr. 8, 1-3)

This is the ὁδός of the ἐόν.

With this way the discourse is closed. Parmenides could have concluded his Poem right here. Being and appearance-phenomenon, science and opinion, and the destiny of mankind, on these very propositions has been built all of philosophy and metaphysics to come.

Thousands and thousands of pages have been accumulated, with exegeses, essays of different nature and import, concepts superimposed on the thought of the thought, and so on. They have fed philosophical discourse which is also quite interesting.

Yet Truth is *Simple* (ἁπλόος, reduction to the One-simple). Parmenides' Poem is extremely Simple and also comprised of a few sentences, with continuous repetitions to make them penetrate, not just in the mind, we believe, but in the "heart" of the reader, so as to make him qualified to open the "door" and be introduced from the sensible to the intelligible. The entity has, in fact, within himself the possibility to solve opinative knowledge, for he is the child of Noûs and therefore of Being (Fr. 1, 10-11).

8

       μόνος δ' ἔτι μῦθος ὁδοῖο
λείπεται ὡς ἔστιν· ταύτηι δ' ἐπὶ σήματ' ἔασι
πολλὰ μάλ', ὡς ἀγένητον ἐὸν καὶ ἀνώλεθρόν ἐστιν,
ἐστι γὰρ οὐλομελές τε καὶ ἀτρεμὲς ἠδ' ἀτέλεστον·
οὐδέ ποτ' ἦν οὐδ' ἔσται, ἐπεὶ νῦν ἔστιν ὁμοῦ πᾶν,   5
ἕν, συνεχές· τίνα γὰρ γένναν διζήσεαι αὐτοῦ;
πῆι πόθεν αὐξηθέν; οὐδ' ἐκ μὴ ἐόντος ἐάσσω
φάσθαι σ' οὐδὲ νοεῖν· οὐ γὰρ φατὸν οὐδὲ νοητόν
ἐστιν ὅπως οὐκ ἔστι. τί δ' ἄν μιν καὶ χρέος ὦρσεν
ὕστερον ἢ πρόσθεν, τοῦ μηδενὸς ἀρξάμενον, φῦν;   10
οὕτως ἢ πάμπαν πελέναι χρεών ἐστιν ἢ οὐχί.

Fragment 8

[It follows that] only one discourse is left about the Way (ὁδός) that it is. On this way there are revealing signs in great numbers: ὡς ἀγένητον ἐὸν ἐστιν: that Being is non-born, ἀνώλεθρόν incorruptible,
in fact it is in its entirety whole (οὖλον), immobile[10]
5   and without end (ἀτέλεστον). Nor was it ever, nor will it be, since it is now[11] all together one (ἕν = thus non many), continuous (συνεχές)[12].
Which birth (γέννα) for it, in fact, will you be looking for? How and in what way would it have grown? From non-being I will not allow you
neither to affirm it nor to think of it because it is impossible to affirm or to think of
what is not. What necessity would ever have pressed it to
10   be born, earlier or later, if it derives from no-one?[13]
It is thus necessary for it to be altogether, or not at all.

---

[10] For the Notes to Fragment 8, refer to page 106 and following.

οὐδέ ποτ᾽ ἐκ τοῦ ἐόντος ἐφήσει πίστιος ἰσχύς
γίγνεσθαί τι παρ᾽ αὐτό· τοῦ εἵνεκεν οὔτε γενέσθαι
οὔτ᾽ ὄλλυσθαι ἀνῆκε Δίκη χαλάσασα πέδῃσιν,
ἀλλ᾽ ἔχει· ἡ δὲ κρίσις περὶ τούτων ἐν τῷδ᾽ ἔστιν·   15
ἔστιν ἢ οὐκ ἔστιν· κέκριται δ᾽ οὖν, ὥσπερ ἀνάγκη,
τὴν μὲν ἐᾶν ἀνόητον ἀνώνυμον (οὐ γὰρ ἀληθής
ἔστιν ὁδός), τὴν δ᾽ ὥστε πέλειν καὶ ἐτήτυμον εἶναι.
πῶς δ᾽ ἂν ἔπειτ᾽ ἀπόλοιτο ἐόν; πῶς δ᾽ ἄν κε γένοιτο;
εἰ γὰρ ἔγεντ᾽, οὐκ ἔστ(ι), οὐδ᾽ εἴ ποτε μέλλει ἔσεσθαι.   20
τὼς γένεσις μὲν ἀπέσβεσται καὶ ἄπυστος ὄλεθρος.
οὐδὲ διαιρετόν ἐστιν, ἐπεὶ πᾶν ἐστιν ὁμοῖον·
οὐδέ τι τῇ μᾶλλον, τό κεν εἴργοι μιν συνέχεσθαι,

Nor from Being will the vigor of a certitude[14] allow that
anything be born which be close[15] to it, therefore neither
to be born
nor to perish granted to it Goddess Δίκη relieving it thence
from shackles,
but she holds it still. Solution to such things lies in this:
it is or it is not (ἔστιν ἢ οὐκ ἔστιν). The decision is therefore
inevitable:
one of the ways must be abandoned, because it cannot
be traveled nor can it be expressed for is the way of the
non-truth,
while the other is, and thus is true [it is the ὁδός that leads
to the ἐόν].
How might Being exist in temporal succession? and how
might it be born?
If in fact it was born, it is not; nor can it be if it will ever
be in the future[16].
So, birth vanished and death waned.
　　　Nor is it divisible since the whole stays identical to
itself[17]
nor can there be anywhere a something more that could
bar its unity

15

20

οὐδέ τι χειρότερον, πᾶν δ᾽ ἔμπλεόν ἐστιν ἐόντος·
τῶι ξυνεχὲς πᾶν ἐστιν· ἐὸν γὰρ ἐόντι πελάζει. 25
    αὐτὰρ ἀκίνητον μεγάλων ἐν πείρασι δεσμῶν
ἔστιν ἄναρχον ἄπαυστον, ἐπεὶ γένεσις καὶ ὄλεθρος
τῆλε μάλ᾽ ἐπλάχθησαν, ἀπῶσε δὲ πίστις ἀληθής.
ταὐτόν τ᾽ ἐν ταὐτῶι τε μένον καθ᾽ ἑαυτό τε κεῖται
χοὕτως ἔμπεδον αὖθι μένει· κρατερὴ γὰρ Ἀνάγκη 30
πείρατος ἐν δεσμοῖσιν ἔχει, τό μιν ἀμφὶς ἐέργει,
οὕνεκεν οὐκ ἀτελεύτητον τὸ ἐὸν θέμις εἶναι·
ἔστι γὰρ οὐκ ἐπιδευές· [μὴ] ἐὸν δ᾽ ἂν παντὸς ἐδεῖτο.
    ταὐτὸν δ᾽ ἐστὶ νοεῖν τε καὶ οὕνεκεν ἔστι νόημα.
οὐ γὰρ ἄνευ τοῦ ἐόντος, ἐν ὧι πεφατισμένον ἐστιν, 35
εὑρήσεις τὸ νοεῖν· οὐδὲν γὰρ ‘ ἢ ’ ἔστιν ἢ ἔσται
ἄλλο πάρεξ τοῦ ἐόντος, ἐπεὶ τό γε Μοῖρ᾽ ἐπέδησεν
οὖλον ἀκίνητόν τ᾽ ἔμεναι· τῶι πάντ᾽ ὄνομ(α) ἔσται,
ὅσσα βροτοὶ κατέθεντο πεποιθότες εἶναι ἀληθῆ,

nor is there a lesser because Being is wholly full of itself[18]

25 it is thus complete entirety of continuity, in fact Being is identical to Being.

Furthermore, unmoving (ἀκίνητον) in the limits of vast bounds[19]

it is without a beginning and without an end since birth and death

have been kept away and excluded from the true certainty. And so it lies identical in its identity, and there remaining

30 in itself it firmly stands. In fact sovereign Ἀνάγκη holds it in the limits of bounds that all around encircle it, for it is by law that Being be a fulfilled;

in fact it lacks nothing, for if it did it would be lacking everything.

The same is for thinking and that for which [οὕνεκεν, in the text] there is thought

35 because without Being whence it unfolds

you will not find thinking[20]. In fact, nothing else either is or will be except for Being, since Moira holds it

to be entire and unmoving. For it will be names all of those things that the mortals decided convinced that they were true:

γίγνεσθαί τε καὶ ὄλλυσθαι, εἶναί τε καὶ οὐχί,   40
καὶ τόπον ἀλλάσσειν διά τε χρόα φανὸν ἀμείβειν.
   αὐτὰρ ἐπεὶ πεῖρας πύματον, τετελεσμένον ἐστί
πάντοθεν, εὐκύκλου σφαίρης ἐναλίγκιον ὄγκωι,
μεσσόθεν ἰσοπαλὲς πάντηι· τὸ γὰρ οὔτε τι μεῖζον
οὔτε τι βαιότερον πελέναι χρεόν ἐστι τῆι ἢ τῆι.   45
οὔτε γὰρ οὐκ ἐὸν ἔστι, τό κεν παύοι μιν ἱκνεῖσθαι
εἰς ὁμόν, οὔτ’ ἐὸν ἔστιν ὅπως εἴη κεν ἐόντος
τῆι μᾶλλον τῆι δ’ ἧσσον, ἐπεὶ πᾶν ἐστιν ἄσυλον·
οἷ γὰρ πάντοθεν ἶσον, ὁμῶς ἐν πείρασι κύρει.

40   to be born and vanish (ὄλλυσθαι), being and not being
the changing of position and mutation of luminous color.
And again, since there is an ultimate limit it is accomplished
like a well-rounded sphere.
Starting at the center and everywhere the same neither
is it necessary that in some way it be larger or smaller in
45   one part or another.
Nor in fact is it possible that a non-being might prevent it
from being in its identity
or is it possible that Being might be more on one side and
less on the other since it all is, inviolable,
therefore it is identical (ἴσον) in all of its parts (πάντοθεν)
and likewise it lies within the bounds [of itself].

Introduction to the world of appearances

Parmenides' cosmological vision as it emerges from the *Fragments* is not only incomplete but of difficult interpretation as well, it is therefore not possible to have a clear representation of the Day-Night process.

However, this cosmology is in the domain of appearances and opinions: appearances as phenomenal world, and opinions as expressions of the sensory subject interpreting the phenomena.

In this domain knowledge is not stable nor does it lead to the end of the journey, since it is in a continuous flux. It is the vision of the mortal who moves "turning the blind sighted eye, and the ringing ear".

«[For them] Being and non-being are deemed the same ... and for them of all things is a way turning in the opposite direction».

(Fr. 6, 8-9)

We refer back again to the «Myth of the Cave» of Plato who drew inspiration from Parmenides. And of Parmenides, for dramaturgical requirements, Plato devised the famous "parricide" (see, *Sophist*), which he did for emphatic tension as well, and also in order to render the subject more vivid by ascribing certain distinctive qualities to the characters (the Divine Plato was also a dramaturge). In fact, this indisputably brilliant representation has come down to us giving rise to many discussions and interpretations; even if Aristotle did equally the same thing [in his turn, with regards to Plato].

Thus, there are as many opinions as there are beings populating a world. Due to its lack of stability and certainty, every opinion is contradicted by another opinion, because the substantive *foundation* that permeates all possible opinions has not been found.

Day and Night are a polarity representing an "object" of perception. It is the world of names and forms whose nature is time, space and cause, and since it was born it has an end, because it has no aseity.

If Day-Night were a real absolute you would have two absolutes: Being and Day-Night. This is inconceivable and contradictory (refer back to what was said in the Chapter "Being").

If Being were *also* Day and Night they would have to be a-temporal and without end, having as a matter of fact the same nature as Being. If, on the other hand, Day and Night are to be considered as Being, then, according to Parmenides' indications, the latter would have to have movement, birth and end which again does not correspond to the indications Parmenides gives about Being.

If the same entity had only the nature of Day-Night, and since Day and Night are moving in time, it would be completely in a continuum-discontinuum process devoid of autonomous and stable will. However this is contradicted by the fact that the entity, as subject, is distinct from the object (Day-Night) up to the point of influencing its very course.

And again, if the nature of Day-Night and therefore of the entity, from where it comes as body, is of a finite and mortal order, from where then might the idea of immortality, eternity, etc., arise to the entity, since these properties fall neither within the nature of Day-Night nor of the entity itself?

Certain properties can never be conceived or expressed if they are not the nature of an entity whatever dimension it may belong to.

The Day-Night polarity can be considered as *essence* and *substance* from where begins the "play" of becoming, through the creation of forms, or bodies, at the sensible as well as the intelligible level. To say that Day and Night, or Light and Darkness, *are* Being is, therefore, not acceptable, according to the principle of non-contradiction already expressed by Parmenides himself.

As for the mortals: «Being and non-being are deemed the same and not the same» because mortals think of them as two distinct aspects, separate and opposed, thus they postulate two absolute principles.

Therefore:

«...Being and non-being are deemed the same
(ταὐτὸν) and not the same, and for them of all things
is a way turning in the opposite direction»

(Fr. 6, 8-9)

This is precisely the way of opinion that as soon as it
is asserted already instantly it contradicts its own assertion. It is inevitable that feeling and dianoetic thought,
which both are movement, cannot grasp Being that is
beyond movement and appearances. So, movement can
be perceived and therefore time, space and cause, because there is a point, a stable center, an observer, which
is conscious of the movement. If the observer were to
be the movement itself it would be unable to perceive it.

There is an oriental saying that goes: "One cannot
dance upon one's own shoulders". Without the perma-
nent it is not possible to be conscious of the transitory.

One can ask oneself: if Day and Night (manifestation) are not Being, can they be considered the nothingness?

Parmenides himself comes to our help and dis-
pels this doubt: «nothingness is not [neither thinkable
nor intuitable]...», *ex nihilo nihil* is an axiomatic truth
enunciated two thousand five hundred years ago. On
the surface these statements could seem innocuous, yet

they are able to make collapse of many absolute conceptualizations that over time have followed one another.

We would like to repeat what we have said previously. There are some who consider only phenomena as absolute reality (positivists-nihilists). There are others who hold phenomena as nonexistent (idealists). For others the perceptible exists as projection of the entity itself, the thinking subject (solipsists). While there are still others who want to render *real* both Being and the very phenomena and so on, putting themselves in an ambiguous position for which το ἐὸν and φύσις coincide; that is to say, the non-born and the born are the same thing, the a-temporal and the temporal identify with one another. But all this is something irrational (refer to what was stated earlier).

Essentially it is necessary to be free from the pair of opposites, necessary to transcend the yes and the no, what is real from what is unreal, therefore free from the world of *doxa*. As long as one is in a set position any other position is excluded.

True Freedom, supreme Freedom is there when the principial polarity itself, from which all other secondary polarities derive, has been transcended. This implies, from what can be deduced from the vision of Parmenides, to be able to put oneself beyond thought itself (which is the polarity = I and not I). One could say: to put oneself in the all-comprehending Silence in which Being unveils by itself in its eternal present. That this Being be called Being or One, *Brahman*, *Paranirvāṇa*, supreme God, *Tao*, and so on has no importance. It is important not to identify with them, because unfortunately for the sake of defending these words, which are simply nominal references, serious conflicts have ensued.

If one follows Parmenides, everything can be put in its right place with few words. If the Goddess (and let us not forget that Parmenides received the revelation from Δίκη, embodiment of the supreme Truth) spoke of "appearances" it means that these must have some degree of truth. In fact, the Goddess not only spoke of Being but *also* of the world of appearances, hence there are two enunciations to be kept distinct, for they have different characteristics and properties. What degree of truth can be given to the world of appearances? Now, in a preliminary manner, we have to reach an understanding on what is meant by *truth*, and not the various partial truths mentioned by mortals.

The seeking of truth is innate to the human being himself. There is a fundamental "instinct" of the species that drives the search for what is true, and real. Hence the idea of truth cannot be left out of consideration, at the most you can have differing ideas on what is intended by truth.

This is dependent on the peculiar tool of perception which is utilized and, above all, on the state of *consciousness* of whoever postulates truth.

The drama of the mortal does not derive from the fact that there can be different conceptions on what truth is or opinion is (although Parmenides' Being does not exclude one or the other), but because there is a will to impose one's own ideal conception with constraints and even with violence. This can be observed in the scientific, religious, political and cultural fields.

It may also be maintained that the true, authentic philosophy (φίλος = lover of, σοφία = wisdom-knowledge) can resolve such conflicts, because it has as its purpose to search, explore, investigate, and propose without any other aim than that of expressing the highest faculty for the mortal, that of meditating and contemplating:

«And this is the divine philosophy...»[1]

(*Phaedrus*, 239b)

It has already been said that Δίκη speaks about the world of appearances. What is the degree of truth we can attribute to it? For Parmenides, truth can be such if it shows those properties of which we spoke about at length and repeatedly. Having accepted those properties, it can be said that a cloud in the sky which appears and disappears on the horizon of the observing subject can be considered neither real nor nothingness in absolute terms. This statement, however, necessarily refers us to something else.

---

[1] Plato, *All the Writings*. Op. cit.

That is to say that since something is perceived, from the point of view of those properties that have been spoken about it cannot be real because it does not have within itself its own raison d'être. Yet, not being nothingness either, since "nothingness can be neither thought nor talked about", then what the Goddess proposes, through Parmenides, seems to us to be obvious: that the phenomenon has a degree of truth, but is not Being. Hence the name "appearances" in the sense that they are phenomena that appear and disappear on the horizon of the *observing subject*, and this is an observation, a perceptual and conceptual obviousness. Therefore they cannot be nothingness, but neither the ultimate truth, which is Being. Consequently, the opinion of the mortals, about which Parmenides talks, lies in the fact of ascribing to the appearance-phenomenon the absoluteness which it does not have.

On the other hand, making an absolute of an opinion (the relative phenomenon) is already a relative and contingent affirmation. Following Parmenides it could be said: it is an opinion that can be contradicted by another opinion, and so on endlessly.

According to Plato if every opinion is considered true, the opinion of he who maintains the distinction between true and false must be considered equally true.

If someone postulates an opinion as true he has to admit as true also the opinion of he who believes him to be erring. He can therefore consider his own opinion completely false.

«So, in a certain sense, is he [Protagoras] not saying that the way each thing appears to me such is for me, and as it appears to you, such is for you – man are you and man also am I?»[1]

(Theaetetus, 152a)

And proceeding in this way you can go on endlessly never reaching agreement and truth.

According to Aristotle, relativity does not make better what is good already, nor white what is white already (compare with what was said earlier).

Day and Night are by nature temporal, thus they are in the sphere of the contingent. When they disappear, since everything which has a birth also has an end, as also stated by Parmenides (Fr. 19), we are confronted with an absolute void (nihilism) unless we refer to a Reality, as founding aspect, which is and does not become. The same thing is proposed by Plato: becoming *participates* of the Reality of Being, but is not Being.

On the other hand, the human being in order to attain ἀλήθεια must begin from where he is. Unless he wants to stop in the sphere of opinion, but this is not of a true philosophical researcher.

Plutarch in *Adversus Coloten* states:

«Parmenides accepts the two natures but ascribes to one and the other sphere what belongs to each.

---

[1] Plato, *All the Writings.* Op. cit.

He places Being in the Idea of intelligible One because it is eternal, incorruptible and identical to itself
due to the fact that it cannot have differentiations;
while in the sensible he places what is movement.
The criteria on which these two aspects are based
can be seen in the statement: the "firm heart of the
well-rounded Truth", which attains the intelligible
and that which finds itself always in the same identity; and the "opinions of the mortals in which there
is no true certainty" because opinions accept things
that regard movement, affections and differences»[1]

Simplicius himself in the *Commentary on the physics* maintains:

«...[Parmenides] calls this discourse "opinative" and
"deceptive" not because it is totally false, but because it goes from intelligible truth (ἀλήθεια) to phenomenon (φαινόμενον) and to opinative, that is to the
sensible»[22]

From Parmenides' vision you have a clear *deductio*:
that the attention rather than on the object, i.e. Day and
Night, must be put not on the subject who observes. Being cannot be objectified.
    The error is not in the sphere of Day-Night, as object,
but in the sphere of the subject perceiving the object. It is
here where the attention must be put.

---

[1] Plutarchus, *Moralia: Adversus Coloten*, 13, 1114 D.

[2] Simplicius, *In Aristotelis physicorum*, 39, 10.

The *Daimon* makes evident two aspects: on the one hand the world of appearances, to which precise connotations were given, and they are what they should be; and, on the other hand, the mortal who has to interpret that world of becoming. It is in this *interpretation* where the entity commits the error.

Making use of the "blind sighted eye" (that is, the simple and immediate sensory vision), he cannot but see only phenomena, appearances. From his point of view he is right, even if he is committing an error of perspective. Hence there is non-opposition towards such a point of view because in addition to what has been said, opposition implies non-comprehension, and therefore one places oneself on the level of *no*.

He who has integrated the world of appearances (since with the realization of the Being all polarities are integrated and transcended) cannot be opposed to anyone. Another error is that of identifying oneself with fallible opinions to the point of making them crystallized, as result of this habit.

A philosophical researcher, in any case, cannot stop at this outlook, he must go further, past the dianoetic preconceptions. If he goes beyond, he will notice that the error as such is not absolute, and Parmenides proves this with the Enlightenment he had.

When with the immediacy of the senses, the mortal perceives that Day and Night are real, and when using a different "eye", he realizes that his assertion was just an opinion and not *Truth*, where did the error go?

He can understand that that opinion has mutated into "well-rounded truth", which has the virtue of comprehending both Being, in that it is and cannot become other than itself, and the world of appearances, which are born and disappear on the dawning of Being.

So, making use of the "eye" that watches, or sees, he becomes both the one who unveils and the means for the unveiling of what *is*, which coincides with Being, or ultimate Reality.

This *seeing* is the disclosing of the Essence that is behind what appears. What this requires of the entity is to be present to oneself as unity, a total entirety as opposed to the multifarious unfolding of things which *veil* ἀλήθεια and lead to the condition of λήθη, oblivion of oneself as ultimate essence.

This is the "salvation" offered by Parmenides: it is necessary to turn from opinion to noetic intuition. The Eleatic, being a philosopher, starts from the world of opinion of the mortals "who know nothing" and goes on to νόησις that knows how to unveil the "well-rounded truth" (see again Fr. 1, 8-10). The human being has these operative tools but often he uses only one, the one expressing the sensory knowledge, which for him is simpler and natural.

«...but transforming the physical sight with another *reawaken that power which everyone has, but only few use*»

(Plotinus, *Enneads*, I, 6, 8. Italics added)

Here lies the ὁδός of solution; it is necessary to perform a conversion-revolution, περιαγωγή. This is the focal point that must be considered, without which one remains in the sphere of the opinative.

The transition from one *state of consciousness* to another higher one, in a completely objectivistic society, is a revolutionary event; and Parmenides' importance for contemporary life and greatness consists also of this.

In a culture whose "eye" is only of a sensory order there can be no ἀρετή nor παιδεία. This is so, because it is based on profit, egotism and of the suppression of the noetic reason, and it favors the πολιμαθία[1] already condemned by Heraclitus (Fr. 40) and by Democritus himself (*Maxims*, Fr. 64-65). Nor can there be πολιτεία because often such a culture turns into a mixture of ideological lies and of individualized activism, where Δίκη is missing and the πόλις suffers. In other terms what is missing is the foundation of a political, educational and formative *Norm*.

In a society undergoing a crisis of values (κρίσις) Parmenides is there to point out the ὁδός to be followed and the means necessary to journey on it.

The Eleatic, it is maintained, gave his πόλις good laws.

Some of its essential ideas are proposed again as a synthesis for the Poem.

---

[1] Mnemonic erudition of many words.

When, by means of Parmenides' teaching, one rises
to the *consciousness* of Being (ἐποπτεία) one finds that a
certain type of formal thought dissolves, or is reabsorbed,
into what is the "well-rounded", integral knowledge
(γνῶσις). With this knowledge both Being, as the foundation, and what becomes, i.e. the object of the appearing,
are put in their right place. Being illumines all, but no
one illumines it:

«It [the supreme Real] is that through which all is
manifested but It itself is not manifested by anything»

«Realize that very *Brahman* whose splendor illumines the sun and the other stars, but which is not illumined by their light, [that *Brahman*] only through
which this entire [universe] manifests»[1]

(Ātmabodha, 61)

«As appearance these things are originated and will
develop in the future to then have an end»

(Fr. 19)

«Observe with noetic intuition, as absent things
equally are, according to truth, present as well; in
fact you will not be able to cut off Being from the
connection with Being [itself] not in a complete [cos-
mic] dissolution nor when it condensates»

(Fr. 4)

---

[1] Śaṅkara, *Ātmabodha*. Op. cit.

«...He will, all of a sudden, perceive a Beauty in its nature stupendous and precisely that, oh Socrates, for which all the earlier pains were endured, that which is first of all eternal, which does not become and does not perish, does not grow and does not diminish»[1]

(Plato, *Symposium*, 210e-211a)

It is not necessary to leave the world of appearances and this is taught to us by Parmenides. He himself never abandoned the world and was in fact of great benefit also to his Polis. However it is necessary to know how to travel through the world as a simple witness, free from the succession of the changing and mechanical processes of appearance. In the East one would say: to be in *māyā* but not of *māyā* or, again, to be in the world but not of the world, as it is taught by the Christian Scriptures.

---

[1] Plato, *Complete Works*. Op. cit.

8 (contd.)

ἐν τῶι σοι παύω πιστὸν λόγον ἠδὲ νόημα   50
ἀμφὶς ἀληθείης· δόξας δ᾽ ἀπὸ τοῦδε βροτείας
μάνθανε κόσμον ἐμῶν ἐπέων ἀπατηλὸν ἀκούων.
    μορφὰς γὰρ κατέθεντο δύο γνώμας ὀνομάζειν·
τῶν μίαν οὐ χρεών ἐστιν ᾗ ἐν ὧι πεπλανημένοι εἰσίν ᾗ
τἀντία δ᾽ ἐκρίναντο δέμας καὶ σήματ᾽ ἔθεντο   55
χωρὶς ἀπ᾽ ἀλλήλων, τῆι μὲν φλογὸς αἰθέριον πῦρ,
ἤπιον ὄν, μέγ᾽ [ἀραιὸν] ἐλαφρόν, ἑωυτῶι πάντοσε
τωὐτόν,
τῶι δ᾽ ἑτέρωι μὴ τωὐτόν· ἀτὰρ κἀκεῖνο κατ᾽ αὐτό
τἀντία νύκτ᾽ ἀδαῆ, πυκινὸν δέμας ἐμβριθές τε.   60
τόν σοι ἐγὼ διάκοσμον ἐοικότα πάντα φατίζω,
ὡς οὐ μή ποτέ τίς σε βροτῶν γνώμη παρελάσσηι.

Fragment 8 (contd.)

50   Here I will end the discourse that responds to certainty and thought
around truth; from here on the opinions of the mortals
you must learn listening to the order of my persuasive
(ἀπατηλὸν) words[21].
The mortals have named two elements
making them separate, and here is where they strayed:
55   they conceived them as separate in their structure and
divided the distinctive signs
from one another: on one side the eternal fire of the flame
which is gentle, light in all identical to itself in every direction
while it is not identical to the other,
but as opposed to the other they put it by itself:
60   Night devoid of light, dense and heavy structure.
This order of the world to you similarly [ἐοικότα, in the text] I entirely expound
so that no credence of the mortals may lead you astray.

---

[21] For the Notes to Fragments, 8 (contd.) and following, refer to page 111.

9

αὐτὰρ ἐπειδὴ πάντα φάος καὶ νὺξ ὀνόμασται
καὶ τὰ κατὰ σφετέρας δυνάμεις ἐπὶ τοῖσί τε καὶ τοῖς,
πᾶν πλέον ἐστὶν ὁμοῦ φάεος καὶ νυκτὸς ἀφάντου
ἴσων ἀμφοτέρων, ἐπεὶ οὐδετέρωι μέτα μηδέν.

10

εἴσηι δ᾽ αἰθερίαν τε φύσιν τά τ᾽ ἐν αἰθέρι πάντα
σήματα καὶ καθαρᾶς εὐαγέος ἠελίοιο
λαμπάδος ἔργ᾽ ἀίδηλα καὶ ὁππόθεν ἐξεγένοντο,
ἔργα τε κύκλωπος πεύσηι περίφοιτα σελήνης
καὶ φύσιν, εἰδήσεις δὲ καὶ οὐρανὸν ἀμφὶς ἔχοντα
ἔνθεν [μὲν γὰρ] ἔφυ τε καὶ ὥς μιν ἄγουσ(α)   5
                              ἐπέδησεν Ἀνάγκη
πείρατ᾽ ἔχειν ἄστρων.

Fragment 9

And since the whole of things is named Light and
Night (darkness)
and both, according to their power, are assigned to these
things or to those
everything equally is full of Light and dark Night
both even because neither with one nor with the other is
the nothingness[22].

Fragment 10

You will learn to know (εἴσηι) the nature of ether
and in ether all
the stars, and from the pure and resplendent lamp of the sun
the consuming (ἀίδηλα) action and where it originated from
and you will know the rotating action of the round-eyed moon
and its nature (φύσις); and you will know too whence
the heavenly vault, that all encircles,
originated and how Ἀνάγκη lead it and held it
imposing the boundaries to the heavenly bodies.

11

πῶς γαῖα καὶ ἥλιος ἠδὲ σελήνη
αἰθήρ τε ξυνὸς γάλα τ᾽ οὐράνιον καὶ ὄλυμπος
ἔσχατος ἠδ᾽ ἄστρων θερμὸν μένος ὡρμήθησαν
γίγνεσθαι.

12

αἱ γὰρ στεινότεραι πλῆντο πυρὸς ἀκρήτοιο,
αἱ δ᾽ ἐπὶ ταῖς νυκτός, μετὰ δὲ φλογὸς ἵεται αἶσα·
ἐν δὲ μέσωι τούτων δαίμων ἣ πάντα κυβερνᾶι·
πάντα γὰρ ῾ ἣ ᾽ στυγεροῖο τόκου καὶ μίξιος ἄρχει
πέμπουσ᾽ ἄρσενι θῆλυ μιγῆν τό τ᾽ ἐναντίον αὖτις   5
ἄρσεν θηλυτέρωι.

Fragment 11

... How earth and sun and moon
the all-enveloping ether and the heavenly Milky Way,
and Olympus,
the highest, and the burning power of the stars moved
towards appearing[23].

Fragment 12

The narrower crowns were filled with pure fire,
the next ones of Night just with a portion of fire;
and at the center of them, is a Δαίμων directing the all:
for everywhere she urges on to laborious[24] birth and
union
5   sending female to unite with male and conversely
male with female[25].

13

πρώτιστον μὲν Ἔρωτα θεῶν μητίσατο πάντων ...

14

νυκτιφαὲς περὶ γαῖαν ἀλώμενον ἀλλότριον φῶς

15

αἰεὶ παπταίνουσα πρὸς αὐγὰς ἠελίοιο

Fragment 13

She [the Δαίμων] conceived²⁶ Eros first among all the Gods.

Fragment 14

Resplendent at night, in need of Light, which comes to it from other [goes] wandering around the earth.

Fragment 15

...always turning the gaze at the rays of the sun²⁷.

15 A

ὑδατόριζον

16

ὡς γὰρ ἕκαστος ἔχει κρᾶσιν μελέων πολυπλάγκτων,
τὼς νόος ἀνθρώποισι παρίσταται· τὸ γὰρ αὐτό
ἔστιν ὅπερ φρονέει μελέων φύσις ἀνθρώποισιν
καὶ πᾶσιν καὶ παντί· τὸ γὰρ πλέον ἐστὶ νόημα.

17

δεξιτεροῖσιν μὲν κούρους, λαιοῖσι δὲ κούρας...

Fragment 15 A

[And the Earth]... has roots in water.

Fragment 16

As in fact time after time occurs the blending
in the articulated organs
so manifests thought (νόος) in men; for it is always the same
in all and in the individual which thinks the nature of
the organs.
Fullness is thought[28].

Fragment 17

...males on the right, and females on the left[29].

18

femina virque simul Veneris cum germina miscent,
venis informans diverso ex sanguine virtus
temperiem servans bene condita corpora fingit.
nam si virtutes permixto semine pugnent
nec faciant unam permixto in corpore, dirae
nascentem gemino vexabunt semine sexum.

19

οὕτω τοι κατὰ δόξαν ἔφυ τάδε καί νυν ἔασι
καὶ μετέπειτ᾿ ἀπὸ τοῦδε τελευτήσουσι τραφέντα·
τοῖς δ᾿ ὄνομ᾿ ἄνθρωποι κατέθεντ᾿ ἐπίσημον ἑκάστωι.

Fragment 18

When man and woman together mix the seeds of
Venus,
and the vital force created in the veins from different
blood shapes well organized bodies, the right balance
is kept.
If then, after the mixing of the seeds, the strengths
oppose one another
they are not able to form a unity in the body
and the sex [body] that is born, from both seeds, [will
be] suffering[30].

Fragment 19

As appearances, these things are originated and will
develop in the future to then have an end;
and the mortals (ἄνθρωποι) have put a name (ὄνομα) on
each [of them] as distinctive sign [ἐπίσημον, in the text].

In conclusion, it can be said that Parmenides' teaching is aimed at making us comprehend what the error consists of into which the mortals fall; error generator of great conflicts and pains. Parmenides has given us an ὁδός-path to travel, so that by following it we can solve the error, and unveil the true and noetic Knowledge inspirer of the reality of Being.

In the light of this perspective one is able to say, together with many lovers of the Eleatic school, that the divine Poem of Parmenides is certainly a message of salvation.

NOTES TO THE FRAGMENTS

¹ The truth that the Goddess offers must refer to that of the Intelligible world, of Light, while that of the sensible world belongs to the δόξα (Fr. 1, 10-12). "Well-rounded": the circle is a round circumference, circular, produced by the irradiating point which is without beginning and without end. One can say that the circumference adequately represents the "Well rounded Truth", the total truth, complete hence there is no truth other than the supreme Being. In fact, the circle (and also the "round Stone") correctly expresses the idea of Infinite.

«...Wherefore he made it round in the form of a sphere extending itself from the center to its extremes in every direction equidistant, that is to say the most perfect of all figures and the most like itself: for he considered that the like is infinitely more beautiful than the unlike»¹

(*Timaeus*, 33b)

[Fr. 1, verse 29 – pg. 47]

² "That which is" in order to be such, must find itself outside of time, space, and cause. Something that appears and disappears, that now *is* but then *is not* any longer, cannot be considered real; it only can be defined as phenomenon, appearance, and devoid of aseity.

---

¹ Plato, *All the Writings*. Op. cit.

This supreme truth is outside of any dianoetic thinking, and needs no demonstration. Being is and cannot not be, and one need not go any further; other ways are untenable. Also the *Ṛṣi* Gauḍapāda[1] states the same things; there is only one way, one supreme Reality: the non-born (*aja*) *Brahman*, beyond any possible category which the empirical mind may conceptualize or conceive; all the rest is "phenomenon-appearance".

These first Fragments are the synthesis of the entire Poem.

[Fr. 2, verse 7 – pg. 49]

[3] Plotinus referring to Parmenides says:

«Thinking and Being are the same thing»

(Plotinus, *Enneads*, V, 1, 8)

On the other hand, if Being were not, thought would not be there either. The latter finds its raison d'être in Being, but Being, complete in its fullness, is beyond thought itself. If Being had to resort to thought (which is movement) in order to be, it would fall into necessity.

Knowledge must resolve itself into pure Being, that is to say it must be cathartic.

[Fr. 3, verse 1 – pg. 51]

[4] Or alternatively: «far away things are equally near (παρεόντα)».

---

[1] See, Gauḍapāda, *Māṇḍūkyakārikā*, IV, 60. Op. cit.

The unity of the ἐòv cannot be touched not even in the face of the succession of the cosmic cycles of dissolution and condensation. The ἐòv is, and does not become, it is a *plenum*, a *continuum*, therefore is beyond contingent properties. If Being is not a source of division, since it is homogeneous in a non-spacial *continuum*, that which the senses regard as the far and the near, as real data as opposites to one another, then with noetic intuition or illumination, truth would emerge by itself. In a metaphysical vision of Being, such as that of Parmenides, there cannot be a before and an after, a far and a near, an above and a below, ἀπεόντα and παρεόντα, and so on, all these things belong to the world of names and forms or to empirical knowledge.

«Considering all entities without birth, consequently there is no place for notions such as eternal and non eternal»[1].

(*Māṇḍūkyakārikā.* IV, 60)

[Fr. 4, verse 2 – pg. 51]

5 The point of arrival is the same as the point of departure. The cosmic cycles have a circular, not linear, time. Each instant is departure and arrival. Alpha and Omega coincide. This Fragment can be considered as surpassing and solving the Pythagorean theory of the "discontinuity of points". This implies that Being is all unity, homogeneity. It is a *continuum*, not a discontinuum, since this pertains to appearance. Nor is there divisibility since everything is the same. There are neither a more nor a less that can be imposed on Being destroying its fullness, or its Entire.

---

[1] Gaudapāda, *Māṇḍūkyakārikā*. Op. cit.

And further, in homogeneity, unity, in which all is full, the origin of something cannot be found, be it even Day and Night; nor can the birth or the beginning of some event be established in a temporal way because that a-temporal *continuum* does not allow any causal modification. If τὸ ἐὸν had a beginning it would also have an end.

[Fr. 5, verse 2 – pg. 53]

⁶ The "two-headed" men identify what is with that which is not, without distinguishing Being from phenomenon-appearance; or, on the other hand, they state that they are not the same thing, «...and for them of all things there is a way turning in the opposite direction».

The opinions of the mortals do not rest on ἀλήθεια because they show contradictory aspects. An opinion of a moment is contradicted in the next. A certain piece of knowledge which is valid today, may turn out to be an error tomorrow.

Human beings are continuously drawn to make judgments that are always partial.

Taking this Fragment 6 into consideration, three positions can be noted:

1. Being is and cannot not be (vs. 1)

2. Non-being, or nothingness (τὸ μηδὲν) as such cannot be, nor can you ever think of what is not (vss. 2-3)

3. The opinion of the mortals who follow the way of the Night, and with their mind experience a contradictory world of "appearances", of phenomena, lacking in that stability and certainty which is, on the contrary, offered by noetic knowledge.

And thus Δίκη teaches not only the ultimate truth ἀλήθεια, but also the relative "truth" of change and of non-abso-
luteness. The two forms are not opposing one another, as
Day and Night are not opposing one another, since they are a
polarity, but one is superior to the other. The irreducible opposition is between the ἐὸν and the μὴ ἐὸν, which corresponds
to the second of the positions above.

These are the fundamental theses of Parmenides' Poem,
and he goes into them in depth in the Fragments that follow.

[Fr. 6, verse 9 – pg. 55]

7 Plato expresses the same thing:

«Now, are not the poets continuously telling us these
things, namely that with the eyes we see nothing sure and
with the ears we hear nothing sure?»[1]

(*Phaedo*, 65 b)

Also Aeschylus, in *Prometheus* (442 and following), says
the same things.

[Fr. 7, verse 4 – pg. 55]

8 ἔλεγκον = refutation, also proof aimed at refutation.

[Fr. 7, verse 5 – pg. 55]

9 If knowledge of the world of sensory experience is not
supported by the faculty of Noûs it remains a deceiving opin-

---

[1] Plato, *All the Writings*. Op. cit.

ion without the possibility of its being resolved in ἀλήθεια. Hence the blind-sighted eye, for it is not the eye of Noûs. Δίκη conversely urges Parmenides to use Logos (λόγωι of vs. 5).

[Fr. 7, verse 5 – pg. 55]

[10] ἀ-τρεμὲς = which does not tremble, is not restless, stays still, which is why any temporal succession is excluded.

[Fr. 8, verse 4 – pg. 63]

[11] νῦν = always present to itself, eternal present. Since Being is beyond any denomination and qualification, when these are used by Parmenides, they are just indications to make one comprehend that Being is not nothingness, it is not an ideal abstraction, it is not time, it is not space, and so on... Being is not something that can be represented, as Day and Night of the second part of the Poem can where, in fact, it is possible to talk about the before, the after, the below and the above, the large and the small, about yesterday and tomorrow, birth and death, and so on. These terminologies are more fitting to the thinking of the mortal.

[Fr. 8, verse 5 – pg. 63]

[12] According to Aristotle:

«...All things are either principle or from principle and of the infinite there is no beginning because it would have an end. Then as principle it is non-generated, because what is generated must have an end [it is our case of Day and Night. Note of the Editor], and the end is character-istic of every dissolution [...]. And the infinite appears as the divine because it is immortal and indestructible, as stated by Anaximander»

(Aristotle, *Physics*, Γ4, 203 b 6)

And again:

«If nothing eternal existed, neither could becoming exist»

(Aristotle, *Metaphysics*, B 4, 999 b 5-6)

Anaximander's infinite, being the ἀρχή of the world and of the worlds, is through which these worlds can be and exist.

The ἄπειρον of Anaximander has divine character, is an impersonal God (θεῖον).

It follows that Anaximander's Doctrine can also be con-sidered of religious order as well as philosophical.

[Fr. 8, verse 5 – pg. 63]

13 The problem of birth and death does not even arise for he who is in the eternal present and in the fullness of what he truly is.

[Fr. 8, verse 10 – pg. 63]

14 Some commentators like M. Untersteiner, and even H. Diels and W. Kranz, use this vulgate ἐκ μὴ ἐόντος, but this is a repetition of vs. 7 in which Parmenides says: οὐδ᾽ ἐκ μὴ ἐόντος.

[Fr. 8, verse 12 – pg. 65]

15 «In That (*Brahman*) which is devoid of parts...»[1]

(*Śvetāśvatara Upaniṣad*, VI, 19)

[Fr. 8, verse 13 – pg. 65]

16 «The birth of a datum that already exists can reasonably be possible only through appearance-*māyā* and not in a real sense.

Whoever believes that things are born in a real sense can only be referring to the birth of what is already born»

«A non-reality cannot be born neither as reality nor as appearance-*māyā*; as an example, the child of a barren woman cannot be born neither in a real way nor through appearance-*māyā*»[2]

(*Māṇḍūkyakārikā*, III, 27-28)

To assert the birth of Being is against reason, to assert the birth of the non-born is a logical absurdity.

«The dualists [those who operate exclusively in the world of appearances] assert the birth of what is non-born. But how can that which is non-born and immortal become mortal?»

«The immortal cannot become mortal, nor the mortal become immortal because there cannot be a change in nature»

«How can a man, who believes that an entity of immortal nature becomes mortal, maintain at the same time that

---

[1] *Śvetāśvatara Upaniṣad*, with Śaṅkara's Commentary. Edizioni Āśram Vidyā, Roma. (Italian edition).

[2] Gaudapāda, *Māṇḍūkyakārikā*. Op. cit.

the immortal, being produced [manifested], still keeps its immortal nature?»[1]

(*Māṇḍūkyakārikā*, III, 20-22)

[Fr. 8, verse 20 – pg. 65]

[17] Being is "identical to itself...because is wholly full of itself".

"Being is, and cannot not be", because a reality which is cannot become a non-reality.

Parmenides expresses an *identity* of "what is entirely whole", outside of determinations or accidents. In metaphysical identity any movement is excluded and indivisible unity is asserted.

[Fr. 8, verse 22 – pg. 65]

[18] The συνεχέια of the ἐόν is excluded if there is a plus or a minus; the ἐόν can neither grow nor diminish.

«This is the eternal greatness of *Brahman*, it does not grow because of action nor does it diminish»[2]

(*Bṛhadāraṇyaka Upaniṣad*, IV, IV, 23)

It must be entirely whole, a *continuum* of being what it is. Plotinus refers to Parmenides' vision when he says:

«...it is not in motion nor is it in stillness; it is not in a space nor in a time, it [unity]...is alone in itself, all en-

---

[1] *Ibid.*

[2] *Bṛhadāraṇyaka Upaniṣad. Op. cit.*

closed in itself....   He [the One] is ineffable, indescribable...he who talks exactly should say of Him: not this, nor that»

(Plotinus, Enneads, VI, 9, III)

This corresponds to the "*neti-neti*": "not this, not this" of *Vedānta*.

[Fr. 8, verse 24 – pg. 67]

[19] Within its limits because it is Alpha and Omega of itself, therefore entire. It can be said, in the infinite radius of itself there cannot be other than itself. In its "ultimate limit it is accomplished" (vs. 42).

Plotinus referring to Parmenides' vision:

«Precisely because the essence of the One is generating all things, it is none of them: therefore it is not "something", nor is it quality, nor quantity, nor Intelligence or Soul. It is not in movement nor in stillness either; it is not in a space nor in a time; it is in itself solitary, all enclosed in itself or, better, it is the formless before every form, before movement and stillness...»

(Plotinus, Enneads, VI, 9, III)

[Fr. 8, verse 26 – pg. 67]

[20] Being is the foundation of thinking and therefore of knowledge. Without Being there could be neither knowledge nor he who thinks or the object of thought.

[Fr. 8, verse 36 – pg. 67]

²¹ ἀπατηλός: deceptive, persuasive, words that convince.
[Fr. 8, verse 52 – pg. 87]

²² Both Light and Darkness, to which these names are given, have alike their metaphysical foundation in Being. However while the ὁδός of Light-Day leads to Being, the other leads to the world of appearances and opinions.

The error is considering Day and Night, which are a polarity, separate and opposed, or considering Day and Night identical to Being, thus contravening to the principle of non-contradiction. It is also an error to put Day and Night as opposed and completely disconnected from Being, creating between Being and the cosmos an unbridgeable duality and conferring to the cosmos a raison d'être of its own, which it does not have.

It can be said that manifestation is a unity at various vibratory levels.

[Fr. 9, verse 4 – pg. 89]

²³ It can be noted how the birth of the world has taken place in time and unravels over time, whereas Being is non-born.

Regarding this Simplicius, in the *De coelo*[1] expresses himself in this way:

«Parmenides concerning the sensible world presents the birth of things that appear and that have an end up to the state of the animals»

---

[1] Simplicius, *In De coelo Aristotelis,* 559, 22-25.

Is it possible to have knowledge of the "appearing" of Day and Night? In order to determine the birth of something the sensory mind needs two terms of relation to move from. In order to determine *when*, for example, one goes from A to B, but if A is not there, what is missing is that *prius* for postulating a *post quem*. If time has been devoured, swallowed by the a-temporal, how can the "when" of birth and death be established?

[Fr. 11 – pg. 91, verse 3]

24 στυγερός = painful, unhappy.
[Fr. 12, verse 4 – pg. 91]

25 The crowns within the cosmos possess fire at the pure state because they have simple elements. As the crowns move to the periphery they contain less of simple fire and more of heavier and compound elements, they therefore solidify, and gets colder. It can also be said that these peripheral crowns are not the brilliant and resplendent stars, but planets as far down as the moon that wanders around the earth, to whom light derives from another.

In a few words Parmenides delineates the principle, not to be underestimated, which supports the world of the stars and the planets. The simple and pure fire is in the middle of the stars like our sun, while the rest has less fire allowing for the solidifying of a planetary form. The moon has no fire, it is an extinguished planet and receives the fire from another; and so where the fire is missing, there is death. It can be said that Parmenides considers the world, and the worlds, substantiated of *light* at various levels of condensation.

The all is permeated by ether which is the basis and the essential foundation giving to fire the possibility to ignite. As Being is the foundation of all that exists, so the all-pervasive ether of the cosmos is the foundation on which rest the stellar and planetary "crowns". Ether has the same function "*prana*" has in the *Vedānta* Tradition. Also *prana* permeates the entire formal manifestation; in fact, in some *Upaniṣad* it is assimilated to the supreme *Brahman*, naturally respecting their different functions.

At the center of manifestation is the *Daimon* Δίκη, who is the *Daimon* of necessity, of the cosmic order so that everything stays in its right place. From this point of view Δίκη is also *Logos*. She is the One who Orders the worlds and at the same time She who gives the initiation to the supreme knowledge. She is the Divinity that starts the world of names and forms.

It is interesting to recognize that, if at the center there is Δίκη, which is intelligence-Logos, the universe, or the appearance, is not the fruit of chance but is guided by a regulating principle, which underlies the entire manifestation. Because of this Parmenides can say that «..there is a *Daimon* that directs the all». This means that She has the power to govern and direct the entire formal life, urging on to union the various polarities of the macro and microcosm, giving life to the manifestation. She is the Great Universal Mother of all Traditions.

Hence one can recognize that, in its substratum, every crated thing contains an intelligent factor. Therefore every entity, which is a part of Day-Night, is not isolated but connected with other entities depending on the dimension and degree to which they may belong.

In other words, manifestation, although appearance, constitutes a unity and therefore there is a cosmocentric rather than an anthropocentric vision.

There is a passage of the *Kaṭha Upaniṣad* (I, I, 15) in which Mṛtyu, the God of Death: «expounded to him [Naciketas] that Fire which is the origin of the world...».

[Fr. 12, verse 6 – pg. 91]

²⁶ The two principles Light and Night are the initial, and substantial primeval cause (πρώτιϛτος or αἴτιον) of manifestation, at the simple and undifferentiated state.

The *Daimon* that governs the existing urges on "...to laborious birth and union" of the negative-positive polarity at cosmological level and up to the anthropological level, hence the generation of multiplicity. The union of the two principles creates a third factor which is the principial seed of manifestation. The *Daimon*, central and causal power of the world, pushes Eros, dynamic and driving power, to begin the generative process. It can say that the "laborious birth" is the fruit of "desire", of the thirst for experiences. The same can be said for the anthropological level.

The manifold cannot be in a state of order if it is not supported by the *Daimon*-Unity which stays still on itself as unity, without modification, otherwise she would not be able to support and govern the formal multiplicity. The principle of every action must be immobile. For Aristotle the first mover is unmoved.

Further, should the ultimate principle, Δίκη, whence the generative process begins (Day-Night), find itself in a changeable condition another principle should be sought that explains and gives raison d'être to that principle which would not be final, but a simple effect, and so on without end.

It can be said that Parmenides presents a cosmogonic aspect, world of names and forms, an ontological aspect represented by the *Daimon* Δίκη who orders and gives the start to the manifest, and a typically pure metaphysical founding factor of all.

[Fr. 13, verse 1 – pg. 93]

²⁷ The reference is to the moon whose light derives from other, i.e. from the Sun. Whereas the earth has roots in the water and the water does not seem to be referred to as ἀρκή of all things, but probably to the representation of Oceanus or again that the earth is surrounded by the oceans.

[Fr. 15, verse 1 – pg. 93]

²⁸ A difficult verse to read which has prompted many interpretations, at times even opposing one another.

Anyhow here are a few "opinions".

Depending on what predominates in the mixing (κρᾶσις) of the two principles (Day and Night), in the gnoseological field one has either a knowledge (νόος) in closer conforming more to the reality of the ἐὸν or, if there is a moving away from the two Principles, δόξα will ensue; while in the field of φύσις there is a greater quantity of one principle compared to the other. In the latter subsists quantity, in the former quality.

Depending on whether Light or Darkness dominates, you will have ἀλήθεια or δόξα.

[Fr. 16, verse 4 – pg. 95]

[29] It is a firm belief in the ancient Mediterranean culture, but also in certain places nowadays, that the male is formed in the right (δεξιτεροῖσιν) of the female uterus, while the female is formed in the left side (λαιοῖσι). This conviction was also shared by other philosophers.

[Fr. 17, verse 1 – pg. 95]

[30] This Fragment was handed down in Latin form by Caelius Aurelianus of Sicca, in Numidia, in his work: *De morbis chronicis*[1]. Cassiodorus refers to him as an important Latin doctor.

At a cosmological level you have that the union of Day and Night (the principial polarity of manifestation) gives life to the formation of the world of names and forms (Fr. 12). At the anthropological level male and female united form the progeny (as above so below); furthermore, a polar coupling (male-female) creates a well organized and balanced corporeal structure. If the two seeds of the polarity are not able to integrate harmoniously pain and sorrow will ensue.

[Fr. 18, verse 6 – pg. 97]

---

[1] Caelius Aurelianus, *De morbis chronicis*, IV, 9, 16.

BIBLIOGRAPHIC REFERENCE*

Aristotle, *Metaphysics*
Edited by Giovanni Reale
Bompiani. Milano 1993

Heraclitus, *Fragments and Accounts*
Edited by Carlo Diano and Giuseppe Serra
Arnoldo Mondadori Editore. Milano 1980

The Presocratics
The Fragments and the Accounts in the Collection of
Hermann Diels and Walther Kranz
Edited by Giovanni Reale
Bompiani. Milano 2006

Ancient and Intermediate Upaniṣad
Edited by Pio Filippani-Ronconi
Bollati Boringhieri. Torino

Parmenides, *Accounts and Fragments*
Edited by Mario Untersteiner
La Nuova Italia. Firenze 1967

---

* With the exception of, Jean Zafiropulo, *L'École Éléate*, a French
Edition, all Texts are Italian Editions.

Plato, *Complete Works*
Edited by Giovanni Pugliese Caratelli
Translation by Emilio Martini
Sansoni Editore. Firenze 1974

Plato, *All the Writings*
Edited by Giovanni Reale
Bompiani. Milano 2000

Plotinus, *Enneads*
Edited by Giuseppe Faggin
Bompiani. Milano 2000

Zeller-Mondolfo, *The Philosophy of the Greeks
in its Historical Development*
La Nuova Italia. Firenze 1967

Zeno, *Accounts and Fragments*
Edited by Mario Untersteiner
La Nuova Italia. Firenze 1970

Jean Zafiropulo, *L'École Éléate,
Parménide-Zénon-Mélissos*
Société d'Édition "Les Belles Lettres". Paris 1950

* * *

GLOSSARY*

ἀγαθόν (Agathón): *Summum Bonum,* the Supreme Good. The platonic One-Good, the One of Plotinus, Absolute.

ἀγένητον (Agéneton): The Ungenerated, the Non-born.

ἀθάνατος (Athánatos): Immortal.

αἴτιον (Aítion): Cause.

ἀκίνητον (Akíneton): Unmoving.

ἀλήθεια (Alétheia): Truth.

Ἀνάγκη (Anánke): Goddess of Necessity.

ἀνάμνησις (Anámnesis): Reminiscence, remembrance, awakening to the reality of the intelligible, of what one really is.

ἄνθρωποι (Anthropoi): Mortals, men.

ἀνώλεθρόν (Anólethron): Incorruptible.

ἀπατηλός (Apatelós): Deceptive, persuasive, words that convince.

ἄπειρον (Apeiron): Infinite, unlimited.

ἀπλόος (Aplóos): Reduction to the One-simple.

ἀ-πόλλων (A-póllon): Not many, non-dual.

ἀρετή (Areté): Excellence.

ἀρχή (Arké): Archetype, suprasensible "model", principle.

ἀτέλεστον (Atéleston): Immobile and without end.

ἀτρεμής (Atremés): That does not tremble, not agitated, thus a temporal succession is excluded.

βροτός (Brotós): Man as a mortal.

γέννα (Génna): Birth.

γνῶσις (Gnôsis): Knowledge, wisdom.

Δαίμων (Daímon): Deity, Demon, Numen that distributes destiny.

διάνοιᾰ (Diánoia): Rational knowledge, way of thinking. See also ἐπιστήμε (epistéme).

Δίκη (Díke): Goddess representing here the incarnation of the supreme Truth and the principle-cause of manifestation, also in the text: Divine Justice, as universal Order.

δίκρανοι (Díkranoi): Two-headed, in the text.

δοκοῦντα (Dokoûnta): That which appears, appearances.

δόξα (Dóxa): Opinion, a grade of knowledge, knowledge of the sensible world; it includes "conjecture, imagination" εἰκασία (eikasía) and "belief, faith" πίστις (pístis). See also ἐπιστήμε (epistéme).

εἶδος (Eîdos): Idea that underlies the form. See also ιδέα (idea).

εἰκασία (Eikasía): Representation, conjecture, imagination. See also δόξα (dóxa).

ἔλεγκον (Elenkon): Refutation, also proof aimed at refutation.

ἐὸν (Eòn): Being, the One, the Real, the Metaphysical foundation of the all existing, in the text. See also ὄν (On).

ἐπίσημον (Epísemon): Distinctive sign.

ἐπιστήμε (Epistéme): "Science-knowledge" of the intelligible. It includes "rational knowledge" διάνοιᾰ (diánoia) and "pure intellection" νόησις (nóesis). See also δόξα (dóxa).

ἐποπτεία (Epopteía): The highest of the Mystical Initiations.

θεῖον (Theîon): Divinity, impersonal God.

Θέμις (Thémis): Goddess representing Divine Law.

θεορία (Theoría): Inner contemplation.

θεός (Theós): Deity, God, God-person.

ιδέα (Idéa): Being, real being; essence. See also εἶδος (eîdos).

κρᾶσις (Krâsis): Combination, union, the coming together.

λήθη (Léthe): Oblivion.

λόγος (Lógos): Reason, the intellect as principle (as opposed to feeling).

μηδέν (Medèn): Non-being, nothingness.

Μοῖρα (Moîra): Goddess representing Destiny.

μῦθος (Mûthos): Revelation, myth.

νόησις (Nóesis): Pure intellection. See also ἐπιστήμε (epistéme).

νοητός (Noetós): Intelligible.

νόος (Nóos): The thinking.

νοῦς (Noûs): The noetic mind; Intelligence, Intellect; universal Soul.

νῦν (Nûn): Always present to itself, eternal present.

ὁδός (Odós): Way.

ὄν (On): Being. See also ἐὸν (Eòn).

ὄνομα (Onoma): Name, denomination.

ὁρᾱτός (Oratós): Sensible-visible.

οὖλον (Oûlon): A Whole, entirety.

οὐσία (Ousía): Principle, Idea-essence.

περιαγωγή (Periagogé): Conversion-revolution.

παιδεία (Paideía): Instruction, education

πίστις (Pístis): Belief, faith. See also δόξα (dóxa).

πόλις (Pólis): City-state; nation, in modern terms.

πολιμαθία (Polimathía): Mnemonic erudition of many words.

πολῑτεία (Politeía): Constitution or form of government. Title of one of the most important Dialogues of Plato, usually translated as "Republic", though it covers all forms of government.

πολλόν (Pollón): Much, large.

πολλῶν (τῶν) (ton Pollôn): Multiplicity.

πρώτιςτος (Prótistos): The very first, primeval in the text.

σήματα (Sémata): Signs, "indicating signs" in the text.

σοφία (Sophía): Wisdom, knowledge.

στυγερός (Stugerós): Painful, unhappy.

συνεχέια (Sunekéia): Continuity.

συνεχές (Sunekés): Continuous.

φαινόμενον (Phainómenon): Phenomenon.

φϊλία (Philía): Friendship among those who love Knowledge, who are in search of the Divine.

φίλος (Phílos): Lover, friend.

φρόνησις (Phrónesis): Wisdom, prudence.

φύσεως (Phúseos, of the text): Natural Order which corresponds to the vedāntic *Ṛta*.

φύσις (Phúsis): Nature, physis.

χώρα (Kóra): Undifferentiated "matter", the substratum of all forms both at gross and subtle levels.

RAPHAEL

Unity of Tradition

Having attained a synthesis of Knowledge (with which eclecticism or syncretism are not to be confused), Raphael aims at "presenting" the Universal Tradition in its many Eastern and Western expressions. He has spent a substantial number of years writing and publishing books on spiritual experience and his works include commentaries on the *Qabbālāh*, Hermeticism and Alchemy. He has also commented on and compared the Orphic Tradition with the works of Plato, Parmenides and Plotinus. Furthermore, Raphael is the author of several books on the pathway of non-duality (*Advaita*), which he has translated from the original Sanskrit, offering commentaries on a number of key Vedantic texts.

With reference to Platonism, Raphael has highlighted the fact that, if we were to draw a parallel between Śaṅkara's *Advaita Vedānta* and a Traditional Western Philosophical Vision, we could refer to the Vision presented by Plato. Drawing such a parallel does not imply a search for reciprocal influences, but rather it points to something of paramount importance: a sole Truth, inherent in the doctrines and teachings of several great thinkers, who although far apart in time and space, have reached similar and in some cases even identical conclusions.

One notices how Raphael's writes from a metaphysical perspective in order to manifest and underscore the Unity of Tradition, under the metaphysical perspective. This does not mean that he is in opposition to a dualistic perspective, or to the various religious faiths, or "points of view".

A true embodied metaphysical Vision cannot be opposed
to anything. What is important for Raphael is the unveiling,
through living and being, of that level of Truth which one has
been able to contemplate.

Writing in the light of the Unity of Tradition Raphael's
works present, calling on the reader's intuition, precise points
of correspondence between Eastern and Western Teachings.
These points of reference are useful for those who want to approach a comparative doctrinal study and to enter the spirit of
the Unity of Teaching.

For those who follow either an Eastern or a Western traditional line these correspondences help us comprehend how
the *Philosophia Perennis* (Universal Tradition), which has no
history and has not been formulated by human minds as such,
«comprehends universal truths that do not belong to any people or any age». It is only for lack of "comprehension" or of
"synthetic vision" that one particular Branch is considered the
only reliable one. Such a position can but lead to opposition
and fanaticism. What can degenerate the Doctrine is either a
sentimental, fanatical devotion or condescending intellectual-
ism, which is critical and sterile, dogmatic and separative.

In Raphael's words: «For those of us who aim at Realization, our task is to get to the essence of every Doctrine,
because we know that just as Truth is one, so Tradition is one
even if, just like Truth, Tradition may be viewed from a plural-
ity of apparently different points of view. We must abandon
all disquisitions concerning the phenomenal process of becoming, and move onto the plane of Being. In other words:
we must have a Philosophy of Being as the foundation of our
search and of our realization»[1].

---

[1] See, Raphael, *Tat tvam asi*, That thou art, Aurea Vidyā, New York.

Raphael interprets spiritual practice as a "Path of Fire". Here is what he writes: «...The "Path of Fire" is the pathway each disciple follows in all branches of Tradition; it is the Way of Return. Therefore, it is not the particular teaching of an individual nor a path parallel to the one and only Main Road... After all, every disciple follows his own "Path of Fire", no matter which Branch of Tradition he belongs to».

In Raphael's view, what is important is to express through living and being the truth that one has been able to contemplate. Thus, for each being, one's expression of thought and action must be coherent and in agreement with one's own specific *dharma*.

After more than thirty-five years of teaching, both oral and written, Raphael is now dedicating himself only to those people who wish to be "doers" rather than "sayers", according to St. Paul's expression.

Raphael is connected with the *maṭha* founded by *Śrī Ādi* Śaṅkara at Śṛṅgeri and Kāñcipuram as well as with the Rāmaṇa Āśram at Tiruvannamalai.

Founder of the Āśram Vidyā Order, he now dedicates himself entirely to spiritual practice. He lives in a hermitage connected to the *āśram* and devotes himself completely to a vow of silence.

* * *

May Raphael's Consciousness, expression of Unity of Tradition, guide and illumine along this Opus all those who donate their *mens informalis* (non-formal mind) to the attainment of the highest known Realization.

PUBLICATIONS

Books by Raphael
published in English

At the Source of Life
Aurea Vidyā, New York

Beyond the illusion of the ego
Aurea Vidyā, New York

Essence and Purpose of Yoga
The Initiatory Pathways to the Transcendent
Element Books, Shaftesbury, U.K.

Initiation into the Philosophy of Plato
Aurea Vidyā, New York

Orphism and the Initiatory Tradition
Aurea Vidyā, New York

Pathway of Fire, Initiation to the Kabbalah
S. Weiser, York Beach, Maine, U.S.A.

The Pathway of Non-duality, Advaitavāda
Motilal Banarsidass, New Delhi

Tat tvam asi, That thou art,
The Path of Fire According to the Asparśavāda
Aurea Vidyā, New York

The Threefold Pathway of Fire
Aurea Vidyā, New York

Traditional Classics
in English

Śaṅkara, *Ātmabodha**, Self-knowledge. Aurea Vidyā , New York

Śaṅkara, **Drigdriśyaviveka***, Discernment between *ātman* and non-*ātman*. Aurea Vidyā, New York

Gauḍapāda, **Māṇḍūkyakārikā***, The Māṇḍūkya Upaniṣad with the verses-*kārikā* of Gauḍapāda and Commentary by Raphael. Aurea Vidyā, New York

Parmenides, **On the Order of Nature**, Περί φύσεως**, For a Philosophical Ascesis. Aurea Vidyā, New York

Śaṅkara, **Vivekacūḍāmaṇi***, The Crest-jewel of Discernment. Aurea Vidyā, New York

Forthcoming Publications
in English

Patañjali, **The Regal Way to Realization***, Yogadarśana

Śaṅkara, **Aparokṣānubhūti***, Self-realization

Raphael, **The Science of Love**

The Bhagavadgītā*

Bādarāyaṇa, **Brahmasūtra***

Five Upaniṣads*, Īśa, Kaivalya, Sarvasāra, Amṛtabindu, Atharvaśira

* Translated from the Sanskrit, and Commented, by Raphael
** Edited by Raphael

Aurea Vidyā is the Publishing House of the Parmenides Traditional Philosophy Foundation, a Not-for-Profit Organization whose purpose is to make Perennial Philosophy accessible.

The Foundation goes about its purpose in a number of ways: by publishing and distributing Traditional Philosophy texts with Aurea Vidyā, by offering individual and group encounters and by providing a Reading Room and daily Meditations at its Center.

* * *

Those readers who have an interest in Traditional Philosophy are welcome to contact the Foundation at the address shown on the colophon page.

Lightning Source UK Ltd.
Milton Keynes UK
UKOW050044170312

189085UK00001B/102/P